How to Earn a Fortune
and Become Independent
in Your Own Business

How to Earn a Fortune and Become Independent in Your Own Business

Merle E. Dowd

PARKER PUBLISHING CO., INC.   WEST NYACK, N.Y.

Library of Congress
Catalog Card Number: 78-133050

Printed in the United States of America
ISBN-0-13-405571-3
B & P

To our four sons—Jerry, Stephen, Richard, and Timothy—with the hope that business opportunities will continue until the time they are ready for independence.

What This Book
Will Do for You

A business of your own, your dream of financial independence, of becoming your own "boss"—may be closer to realization than you think. By starting and operating a business of your own, you can earn double, triple—up to ten or more times your present earnings. That's what this book is all about—to help you start your own business (or take over someone else's business) and make your own FORTUNE.

Understand, the thrust of this book is—MORE MONEY and INDEPENDENCE. Forget about "psychic income" or "job gratification"—this book aims at getting you into a business that nets you several times your present spendable cash. Along with more money, you can achieve great personal satisfaction from starting and operating a business of your own—but money is the first goal.

In this book you'll learn about systems engineering—a new way of looking at things. With systems engineering, you look at every part of a job from beginning to end. By using these planning techniques, you minimize your chances of failure and maximize your opportunities for earning more money.

Only you can decide whether you have what it takes to "make it big." Some people were born to work for someone else. They perform better under someone else's discipline and direction. Such people should not try to develop their own businesses. But, if you have dreamed the American Dream of earning your fortune in a business of your own, you probably fit into the following picture—

- You are skilled in a marketable skill and are probably well educated.
- You are working now or have worked for a big company and are experiencing a big company's lack of interest in the individual.

7

● You are probably not satisfied with your present earnings. You KNOW your job contributions deserve a bigger cut from the profits. From your own analysis you know you are worth more than your fellow workers who may get just as big a paycheck as you.

● You believe—in fact, you KNOW you could do better on your own—but how?

This is the book that tells you, step-by-step, how you can turn your gnawing discontent into more money—big money—by striking out on your own. But, such a road is far from easy. Starting your own business calls for investments of your time and money now in anticipation of a big return for later. Learning from the experiences of others will help you steer around many of the rocky shoals that have meant disaster for others "going it alone."

This book brings you a factual, common-sense approach—one you can identify with, learn from, and draw inspiration from because it includes many examples of dissatisfied individuals, like yourself. They decided they, too, could "make it big" and did. But, remember, reading one of the numerous books on physical fitness won't make you fit—you must work at the exercises too. So, just reading this book won't automatically set you up in a profitable business. You must put these principles and down-to-earth advice to work. This book is a guide, but you must follow the directions to win.

Don't expect to find shortcuts that border on being illegal, immoral, or unethical as a quickie route to big profits. Such shortcuts seldom lead to long-term riches. And they are outside the concept of this book.

This book will help you learn from the experience of others, from their mistakes as well as their successes. You don't have time to "reinvent the wheel" or to make all the mistakes yourself to learn. So, this book concentrates those ideas which have proved successful for others into one handy volume for your benefit and profit.

Merle E. Dowd

INTRODUCTION

OPPORTUNITIES ARE GREATER THAN EVER FOR STARTING AND OPERATING YOUR OWN BUSINESS

Who says opportunities are shrinking? That there are no longer opportunities for you to start your own business? Take a look at these facts—

● During 1950, 93,000 new businesses opened their doors. But, by 1968 the number of new businesses starting grew to 234,000 in one year.

● Small business is BIG business—1,884,311 businesses in the United States employ three or less persons—including the boss. There are 685,293 businesses with four to seven employees. Companies employing 500 or more persons, in contrast, number only 10,704.

● Franchising (see Chapter 8) accounts for around 600,000 firms. Each year about 40,000 new franchised businesses open.

● Horatio Alger, of past fictional fame, was a piker compared to the new enterprisers who started with borrowed money and an idea and have become millionaires many times over—

—Jack Simplot built an empire based on Idaho potatoes. His personal wealth is currently reported to exceed $200 million, and he is the richest man in all of Idaho

—John D. Macarthur built Bankers' Life & Casualty, along with his own personal fortune now said to be well over $100 million

—Jose Zorrilla, a refugee who arrived penniless from Castro's Cuba, took a job in a plastic molding plant for $165 a week. Within a year and a half, he saved $700, borrowed

9

$1,300, and bought a plastic molding machine to start his new business. Eight years later, his company was turning out $1 million of plastic toys.

About 11 million businesses, including farms, operate in the United States. All but about 11 per cent of these 11 million businesses operate as sole proprietorships and partnerships.

MAKING IT "BIG" BY YOURSELF

Look at these facts—then figure your chances for "making it big" in a business of your own rather than working for a big company.

● Salaries and bonuses paid to the top echelons of company executives are not keeping pace with general business growth, according to an in-depth survey of executive compensation. When you allow for taxes, executives in the 60's earned less than their counterparts in 1940—a year when executive earnings were still down from the effects of the depression in the 30's.

● Only the fringe benefit packages for big executives have kept pace with inflation. Earnings fail to reflect the increase in business volume and profits. Further, the chances for executives to reach top positions declined as a result of mergers and conglomerations.

● Executives reach top positions at an older age and keep their top positions for shorter periods than formerly—so they earn top pay for fewer years. In contrast, the new breed of millionaire entrepreneurs establish their own businesses and accumulate their fortunes before age 40 in many, many cases.

● Stock option plans and favorable stock-purchase opportunities offer big-company executives a chance for capital-gain income, but similar opportunities are much more abundant for the aggressive new-business entrepreneur.

● Security and the promise of income growth, fringe benefits, and retirement credits hold many middle managers in big business. Men who lived through the problems of the depression-ridden 30's opt for security. Yet, big business offers less security than one's own business for capable, skilled managers, because—

● Jobs and functions become obsolete at a rapid pace in

business. The half-life of an engineer is now figured at about ten years. That means, within ten years half of an engineer's knowledge will be obsolete.

● Mergers and conglomerations leave layers of capable managers on the street—often at the peak of their organizational efficiency.

● Government programs (Social Security, unemployment compensation, etc.) provide a "safety net" to catch those who may fall from a jump into a business of their own. So, failure may not be as catastrophic as in earlier years. Losses are chargeable against taxes (government shares loss as well as gain) and the lessened sting of a bankruptcy provide an increased measure of protection for the risk-taking businessman.

MYTHS ABOUT SMALL BUSINESS

Don't be misled by the myths about starting your own business.

MYTH No. 1—No opportunities left—You've already seen that the numbers of new businesses increase faster than population each year.

—Technology spawns new business opportunities faster than entrepreneurs can take advantage of them.

—Franchising firms offer more opportunities than there are takers.

—Major, countrywide problems, like cleaning up our environment, for example, open new opportunities so vast that the size of the business isn't even fully determined yet. But, for starters, the United States government plans to spend $10 billion or more each year to improve our environment.

MYTH No. 2—Big business competition is too tough—Certain kinds of business, autos, steel,chemicals, require huge agglomerations of capital to operate. But, these big businesses hold a price umbrella over small business opportunities in selling and using the products of big business. Auto sales, service stations, repair shops, and parts suppliers support rather than compete with the big auto manufacturers. Construction using steel products, and the many end users of chemical products offer the small businessman ready-made opportunities. The RTE Corporation, for example, makes electrical transformers and competes directly with two giants, General Electric and Westinghouse. But RTE continues to grow and brings in profits higher, as a percentage of investment, than either of its big-business competitors. Consider the more than 30 companies who assemble engines, wheels, and glass fiber bodies of their own designs to build "dune buggies" and the many other ATV's (All-Terrain Vehicles).

MYTH No. 3—Small businesses fail frequently. Statistically, the numbers tend to bear out this generalization. But, a study of 91 new businesses in one state indicated that—

—Forty of the 91 new businesses stopped operations within the first two years of operation for all reasons.

—Twenty per cent of the 40 closures resulted from personal reasons as individual as the owner, a woman, becoming pregnant. Even so, though rated as a closure, the firm was actually sold to another owner and the business continued.

—Most of the 32 other closures failed because they were ill-conceived to start. For example, one entrepreneur opened a small grocery with only $25 worth of stock, intending to increase his stock as profits were earned. Others started a business on a sudden impulse because an opportunity became available even though the new owners had little or no experience. Such ill-conceived and under-financed business openings and quick closures confuse the statistics of small-business success. The following chapters advise you on how you can avoid the obvious pitfalls that lead to failure.

MYTH No. 4—Small businesses return small earnings. Again, statistics can be misleading. Many marginally profitable small businesses continue simply because the owners have no alternative, are unskilled, and will not invest the time and effort necessary to boot-strap themselves into the big-money league. Widespread averages overemphasize the low end of the income scale. Yet, thousands of individuals multiply their earnings and profits into sizeable fortunes.

Men and women who succeed in their own business combine their unique skills, motivation to succeed, no-nonsense planning, competitive spirit, physical stamina and energy with a calculated risk to achieve their goal of money, prestige, and ego satisfaction. Don't be confused about the problems and risks of starting your own prosperous business, they are immense. But, you can succeed if you—

- Offer something unique.
- Compete aggressively with innovation and skill.
- Assume risks that you know and understand.
- Project your combination of skills and managerial abilities with the aim of understanding and pleasing your customers, the "service with a smile."
- Plan your new business start, take each step in time with your plan, and persist despite discouragement and crisis.

The following chapters will aid you in finding your niche and helping you achieve the success you deserve.

Merle E. Dowd

Table of Contents

15

1

Moonlighting--Your Low-Risk Route to Earning Your Fortune

One step at a time—learn as you earn—start small and progress at your own pace. That's how moonlighting, the business you work at part-time while holding down your regular job, starts you in business. You learn if you are the type and whether you like managing your own business. When you take the low-risk, moonlighting route to starting your own business, you—

- *Discover the full range of advantages (and problems) that can be yours in a business of your own.*
- *Follow step-by-step the same route others have pioneered to your own fortune.*
- *Learn how to turn moonlighting problems to advantages.*
- *Develop your moonlighting business as a family commitment.*

"I first started out with this little shop in my base-ment . . ." Many a hard-driving business owner started small—in his basement or garage in his spare time. They prospered because they learned the facts of managing their own business while "moonlighting." You, too, can join the new generation of budding fortune hunters - independent "be-your-own-boss" types. By moonlighting, you invest your "sweat equity" to build your own business—to earn your private fortune—to gain independence.

As a moonlighter—you work by day for someone else—and for yourself at night. You'll need a fierce desire to fuel your drive for riches and independence. About two-thirds of the 4 million "multiple job-holders," as the U.S. Department of Labor calls moonlighters, work at another job for a few hours a week to expand their earnings. These government workers, teachers, housewives, and laborers trade time and effort for more money. But, the moonlighters you can learn from are those who are investing their time, energy, savings, and know-how to build a new independent company or business of their own. Here are a few of the reasons you may profit from looking at moonlighting—

● *Money*—You're interested in thousands—or hundreds of thousands of dollars—not a few extra bucks per week. You're looking for the big payoff—the one you'll never find working for someone else.

● *Energy*—You're too itchy to stick in a rut. Your job fails to tax your capacity or is uninteresting—so, you look around for opportunities to spend your excess energy on—building a business that's yours alone.

● *Time*—Along with energy, your job absorbs too little of your time. Cutting the grass, watching TV, fishing, and barbecuing in the backyard get old—so you look for ways to spend your time profitably—with a potential for the big payoff. Besides, time without the money to travel and enjoy yourself can be a bore.

● *Pride*—Part of your burning desire to become independent comes from pride—you don't like being bossed. You want to build and do things YOUR way—You want to manage your own life.

● *Satisfaction*—Big business, computers that convert everything, including people, to numbers, and dehumanizing routine take much of the fun out of working. You can't point to a product and say—"I built that—" or —"That was my idea." So, for satisfaction, for the sense of accomplishment you feel is important, you build a business that's uniquely your own—and you start small, by moonlighting.

● *Chance of Success*—You look at your chances of "making it big" in a big company! Pretty slim—right? Then, you look at the salaries of top executives. Compare the chances of your getting to the top and the rewards if and when you get there and you'll discover chances of making it big are better than ever—OUTSIDE OF BIG COMPANIES. If you're the kind of motivated man or woman who can fight your way up through the multiple layers of big company management, you can probably do better spending the same kind of effort building your own business from scratch or rebuilding a business about to go "belly up." Now—let's see how you can reduce risks through moonlighting.

HOW TO MOONLIGHT YOUR WAY TO A FORTUNE

Arnie Carriloni built his own private fortune by starting and managing a string of pizza places, even though he began his career as an engineer in an aerospace company. Despite his technical education he tired of days bent over a drawing board, a routine that provided little job satisfaction. He could also see an early "topping out"—a salary limited by government contracts. Instead of competing for a management slot, Arnie decided to open a pizza place working part time. He wondered if designing pizzas instead of airplanes would challenge his interest—even if it paid handsomely (as it turned out it did). He worried about losing his technical competency and about wasting the engineering education he had worked his way through college to acquire.

Arnie's logical, engineering approach led him to search out a location near a highway, a big shopping center, and a theater. To save his limited cash, he overhauled a balky used oven. He acquired other equipment on credit.

When he was ready, he opened the shop by spending his vacation installing equipment and remodeling the space. At the end of two weeks he was ready for business–and he returned to his drawing board job. But, every afternoon at 4 o'clock Arnie's wife opened the doors and *Arnie's Pizza* was in business. Arnie dashed to the shop from work to help handle the dinner trade. Many of his orders were for carry-out pizzas. During slow periods of the evening he assembled pizzas and froze them for sale through a local market. On weeknights the shop closed at 10, but on Fridays and Saturdays, Arnie kept open until 2:00 a.m.

By keeping on at his job while starting the pizza place, Arnie found–

● Volume built slowly, so during early weeks, his expenses exceeded income. Even his out-of-pocket cash costs exceeded income the first two weeks. Arnie kept advertising costs low by spotting a number of small ads in neighborhood newspapers. He also posted printed cards at locations frequented by teen-agers. A small ad with a half-price coupon in the local high school newspaper brought in heavy weekend student traffic. Fair prices and yummy pizzas kept early customers coming back, and they spread the word to others. So, volume built with time–but time can be expensive unless you have a job to fall back on during the start-up period.

● *Building business skills*–Despite Arnie's analytical background and the pizza recipes his wife had practiced, he learned that–"Experience in business comes by learning from your mistakes." Arnie paid for his experience in a small way because he started small. Take advertising, for example. The coupon idea, even though it brought in half-price business, allowed him to check which papers produced results. Competitive shopping brought his costs for materials down. He found that he spent too much time trying to keep his own accounts. He logically reasoned that since his time was short, he should spend his hours productively. So, he brought in a Certified Public Accountant (CPA) as a moonlighter from the same aerospace company. The CPA set up a cost-control system that opened Arnie's eyes to further cost reduction possibilities. More important, Arnie could spend more hours working at the shop.

● *Reducing cost for starting*–With his salary to cover his

family's living costs, Arnie could use his savings and borrowed money to start his pizza place. Even with his careful planning, cash demands for rent, payments on rented equipment, materials, advertising, and supplies exhausted his savings. So, he borrowed from a bank which approved the loan mainly because Arnie still worked at his regular job. When the business broke even and then began to return a profit, Arnie kept on working at his job as an engineer. He channeled cash flow from the pizza business to pay off loans first, and then to buy his leased equipment. Only when his debts were completely paid off did Arnie quit his regular job to run the business full time. With no debts and a record of profitable operation, Arnie had no trouble borrowing money to open his second shop.

For Arnie Carriloni, running a business turned out to be far more challenging than designing airplanes—but in a different way. The point is, Arnie couldn't be sure until he actually tried. Now, he owns a string of pizza places and is thinking of franchising others. As for losing his technical training: Dr. A.J. Cronin became world famous and wealthy as a writer after becoming a doctor. Not everyone guesses right the first time.

Arnie's example is repeated over and over every year in the U.S. Our free enterprise system offers opportunity and flexibility. And those opportunities can be yours if you plan ahead, take on only those risks you can afford through moonlighting, and dedicate your time and energy to getting over that big stumbling block—getting started and getting up to speed without going broke.

YOUR STEP-BY-STEP GUIDE TO STARTING YOUR MOONLIGHT BUSINESS

Sure, you'd like to run your own business. You'd like to turn your free time into dollars. You'd like to build for the future with a business you could manage. So, what's stopping you? You can follow these proven steps one by one, with less risk, because you keep your full-time job and moonlight your way to a fortune and an independent business of your own.

Fix Your Objectives

Successful business founders decide on what they want out of a business and then proceed aggressively toward that goal. If you plan to start moonlighting, will your business continue part time? Or, do you aim to build it to a full-time business? If your business begins as an extension of a hobby, are you more interested in pursuing your hobby or developing a business? With either part-time or full-time objectives, you'll find that moonlighters who start their own business—

● Earn money from the limited hours available. Instead of working at a fixed rate per hour, you can benefit from your own ingenuity and skill. If you are a TV repairman working for yourself, you won't waste time locating the trouble and repairing it. You learn fast that your profits depend on your productivity. Every time-saving trick you can find pays off in more income. Your efforts relate directly to the income—the more hours worked, the more income earned. If you need test equipment to cut trouble-shooting time, you study the payoff—should you invest part of your profits in equipment to earn more money later? As a skilled tradesman or craftsman, you can almost always do better working for yourself than you can for wages.

● Enjoy a heady feeling of independence. You'll find you like making decisions on your own. By starting as a moonlighter, you make your share of mistakes without worrying unduly. You'll find you are your own severest critic—worse even than your boss at times.

Find Your Opportunity

Skill, experience, and know-how still underlie every successful business. So, assess your skills. Are you a talented auto mechanic with a knack for finding and correcting troubles with engines, transmissions, and running gear? Can you trouble-shoot electronic gear—television, high-fidelity, and tape-recorder sets? Are you a qualified engineer, accountant, purchasing specialist, or all-around handyman? Regardless of your skill, there's a market for it. And, where there's a market, you can build a business. So, look inward, assess your capabilities as objectively as if you were examining a unique, potential asset—as follows—

● What do you like to do? Do you like fishing and hunting better than working in an office? Art F—did, so he and his wife established their own fishing camp far up in Canada. For five months a year the two of them entertain fishing parties in their austere cabins—furnishing boats, bait, food, and provisions—plus a smoke house to preserve the huge Kamloops trout caught. We all tend to put more effort into jobs we like doing—so search out your real preferences.

● Where do your skills lie? All businesses depend on basic skills plus creative ideas—plus much, much more. But, skill and know-how are essential. Arnie Carriloni's skills consisted of a logical, engineering approach to problem solving along with his wife's pizza recipes and his own chef's experience. If you are an inventor, your idea may promise something unique or an improvement over existing products. Perhaps your hobby provides a unique skill, as Bill Garrison's, for his highly successful Studio 714 (see Chapter 6). If you find you have more than one marketable skill, list them all. Examine each skill and assess its business potential.

● Look for problems to be solved. Chapter 2 concentrates on finding opportunities among problem areas.

● How have others found opportunities? Study the business section of your local newspaper, the *Wall Street Journal,* trade publications, *Business Week* and *Income Opportunities* for ideas. Sometimes a successful idea developed in another area can be adapted for your area.

● Check the many ideas for new businesses in later chapters. The demands for services continue to expand, as noted in Chapter 3. How about a franchise? Chapter 8 tells you how you can find the franchise best for you.

Accumulate Assets

Money, skill, and experience are the assets you need to start your own business. You may already have them all. If so, you're practically ready to start. If you have the skill but need money and experience, you can accumulate these two assets by moonlighting.

● *How to Acquire Money*–The shortest distance between two points may not always be a straight line. You may need to moonlight at a second job to build up the cash you need to start your own business. Savings from your regular job plus earnings from a temporary cash-raising second job build capital much more quickly than just saving out of a single paycheck. Or, maybe your wife works to accumulate cash. Try turning some of your assets into cash–trade your new car for an older one with reliable mileage still to be used, sell a camper, refinance your home (although this method could be costly in times of high interest rates), or sell your house and move to an apartment or trailer. Examine every possibility in detail–cash value of your life insurance, borrowing from relatives or close friends, establishing a line of credit with a bank. (See Chapter 10 for other money-raising possibilities.)

● *How to Acquire Experience*–Working for a successful business lets you soak up methods and operating procedures that obviously work. You can often pick up such experience by moonlighting–working in the kitchen of a fine restaurant during busy weekends, handling evening and weekend calls for service at a marina, repairing television and radio sets, appliances, and sound systems   also   part-time programming for data processing, selling, and many more. The money you make and the skills you develop are bonuses to the experience and practical know-how you acquire during this trial period.

Organize Your Business

Decide right from the beginning whether your new business will be a corporation, partnership, or single proprietorship. Check the advantages of each form of business organization in Chapter 12.

Develop an Operating Plan

The type of business you select affects your planning, but consider these ideas as a minimum–

● Estimate sales, overhead, and purchased services in enough depth to draw up a *pro forma* operating statement. Sales will probably cause you the most trouble in estimating. If necessary, start with a SWEG (for Sweeping Wild-Eyed Guess). Collect every bit of information possible to help you estimate. Arnie Carriloni put his first estimate together after observing patrons in six other pizza places. He noted what they ordered, how many customers came in on different nights, and the amount of each check. Although his figures were not precise, they provided a clue to the gross sales he could expect. You can do the same thing for your idea—estimate the number of customers and the value of each sale—then compute a total.

● Play "Devil's advocate" to pick out flaws in your planning. Consider whether your estimated sales will cover all costs—materials, labor, overhead, taxes, and purchased services. If costs exceed estimated gross sales, you either face a problem or your estimates need refining. Sometimes, at this point you discover your plan simply won't work. Better to flush out these problems before you start than afterward. Suppose you find that your costs exceed estimated gross sales only at first. Arnie Carriloni figured this would happen before he started. But, his plan called for building volume with time. So, consider two operating plans—one while you're starting and one you can live with for the long pull. When your short-range plan projects a loss, as Arnie's did, decide how much cash you will need to carry you through the initial volume-building period.

● Examining operating capital and asset requirements, listing every cost, and totaling your equipment requirements can open your eyes to several problems—

1. When everything you need appears on one list, the dollar total will probably surprise you. But, better to be surprised while you are planning than when you run out of money. Check for opportunities to reduce the cash required— buying used machinery, bartering goods for accounting help, leasing instead of buying equipment, operating out of space in your home instead of renting a shop, or simply borrowing some items from friends for a while.

2. Estimates of operating costs can be just as staggering as the total of assets. Compute your costs in at least two

categories—fixed costs that will vary little with volume and variable costs that go up and down with business volume. Fixed costs include shop rent, equipment rental, some kinds of advertising, licenses, etc. Variable costs include parts, materials, hired labor, and those items that vary with volume. Unless you can estimate your business volume closely, draw up a list of costs for three levels of business volume—an optimistic level, pessimistic level, and a median level. Somewhere in this analysis you'll find the volume you need to break even. Be sure to include a value for your own labor in these calculations. Planning on paper can highlight problem areas quicker than actual operations. Big businesses regularly plan future operations on one- and five-year cycles and check alternative possibilities on computers.

3. Check the breakeven point carefully. When you are moonlighting, your time may limit the business volume you can handle. Businesses that require considerable investment, such as a restaurant, must generate enough volume to spread the fixed costs over many sales. Labor-intensive businesses, such as repairing TV sets, involve few fixed costs, so a breakeven point occurs at low volume. Before you begin, either moonlighting or full-time, you need to recognize the breakeven point where sales cover all fixed and variable costs. Operations over the breakeven point generate profits in addition to your wages.

● Write your plans on paper. Unless you write out each item of your plan, you tend to skip important parts. You need the discipline of working out your business on paper before actually beginning. Arnie Carriloni developed a plan with these parts—

1. Fixed expenses included rent for the store he leased each month, his wife's salary full-time, his own salary part-time, rental fee for the oven, and interest on money borrowed to buy tables, chairs, a refrigerator, and other equipment.

2. Variable expenses included flour, cheese, tomato sauce, and the other ingredients for pizzas, electricity for the oven, wages for extra help on weekends, laundry, and those items expended in serving pizzas.

3. Partially, fixed-variable expenses included advertising,

promotional expense, such as the half-price pizzas, electricity for lighting the store, and maintenance expenses.

4. Some of Arnie's costs were postponable—such as wages for him and his wife. However, unless Arnie considered these costs in the total, he could not analyze the overall profitability of his pizza place at the three volume levels.

Start Your Business

You can study, gain experience working for someone else, accumulate cash, equipment, and know-how, and develop operating plans on paper, but until you actually begin, you will never earn your fortune or gain the independence you're looking for. Begin small—preferably by moonlighting. Figure you'll make mistakes. Your operating plan should include some margin for wrong estimates, your assets will include a kitty of cash for emergencies, and you may work more hours than you planned. But, you'll never learn to swim without getting into the water. Keep your plan flexible, and be prepared to make changes. Compare operating results with your plans as your business progresses. When problems develop, search out the causes and correct them as quickly as possible.

When you start your moonlighting business, you may encounter problems that do not face the full-time entrepreneur. Some of these problems can be turned to advantages, as noted below.

HOW TO TURN MOONLIGHTING PROBLEMS TO ASSETS

As a moonlighter you keep many of your problems small and manageable, but others take their place. Rather than solve the problems unique to moonlighting with "brute force and awkwardness," search out a way to turn minuses (problems) to pluses (assets). Typical of these moonlighting problems and how you can apply innovative solutions include—

Turning Shift Times to an Advantage

Washing machines don't always stop working from 8 to 5

on weekdays. Pipes sometimes spring leaks or drains get plugged at night—or on Sunday afternoon. Boat motors conk out when people are using them—on weekends. Established service businesses usually work regular hours during the week and close weekends or charge fantastic rates overtime. You can take advantage of these time schedules. For example—

● Ernie, an electronic technician, kept sophisticated flight test equipment operating as his regular job. But, he repaired television sets in his spare time. He made many a friend and added to his list of customers by lighting up the tube for a Saturday night movie or for a Sunday afternoon football game. Instead of competing with established repair shops, he aimed for the emergency, out-of-sequence business. He started small by fixing sets for his friends. Inexpensive business cards spread the word around even farther. Established businesses referred emergency calls to him rather than call in an employee at penalty rates. By operating out of his home, he kept overhead low. He found emergency business so profitable, he maintained that approach when he launched his business full time. He took his free time during the day and continued working evenings and weekends. A surprising number of independent businessmen follow this idea of "contrary thinking." That is, they take their days off during the week when ski slopes, golf courses, tennis courts, and fishing grounds are uncrowded. Also, there is less traffic—and less competition. Yet, rates for services fall under the overtime price umbrella, so time yields more profit.

● When people play is time for work when you're catering to the boat owner, skier, bowler, fisherman, etc. If you service the recreational market, weekends generate peak demand. Peter M—was always fascinated with boats. As a teen-ager, he worked part time in a marina. Later he took vocational courses in small-engine mechanics and boat overhaul techniques. Working at a marina paid too little to support his family and was seasonal. So, he took a full-time factory job. On weekends he serviced engines and used a Citizens Band radio to answer emergency calls. Today his business earns enough during the short boating season to support his growing family all year. Now, he is looking for another opportunity to use his spare winter time in another business.

● Establishing a mail-order business activates spare time whenever it is available. Mail orders that come in during the day are easily packaged during evening hours or weekend hours. When Pete decided to establish his own commercial photography studio, he recognized that he couldn't jump into a full-time studio because of his limited capital. So, he specialized in wedding photography. He still works full time at his teaching job while he develops his business volume. Pete plans to work at both jobs until his wedding picture business will support him and his family—then he will expand into commercial photography.

● When workers use their cars for commuting during normal business hours, they need repairs on weekends or during an evening. Your opportunity—set up a repair facility that specializes in off-hours maintenance. You gain another advantage with an off-hours auto-repair or body-repair shop—moonlighting mechanics looking for a second income. Ted S—put himself through college by working at night on professors' cars (see Chapter 3 for operating details).

● Changing shifts to moonlight during normal business hours meets the problem head-on. If your factory operates multiple shifts, change to an odd shift. Your spare time then becomes available during business hours. You'll be "daylighting" instead of moonlighting. When Lloyd G—wanted to start his own interior decorating service, he could gain access to distributor showrooms only from 9 to 4:30 weekdays. As a commercial artist for an aerospace company, he normally worked days plus frequent overtime that disrupted evening appointments. But, by changing to the swing shift, he rarely worked overtime and could call on clients or shop at distributor showrooms during daytime hours.

● Activate wife or teen-agers to make contacts and deliveries during normal business hours. Moonlighting must be an all-family affair to succeed.

—Hang Yii is a talented sound-system specialist. He installs new systems for his employer during the day. Evenings he repairs units brought to his basement workshop at odd times. His attractive wife takes in the troubled sets during the day, records the reported symptoms, and organizes them for Yii to work on later. When a repair calls for some part he doesn't stock, Mrs. Yii picks it up the next day when the wholesaler is open.

—Harry's *Fix-It Shop* operates much like the Yii's.

Harry's wife spends her days at the little shop near a suburban shopping center. Women bring in toasters, irons, and other small appliances for repair during shopping trips. Harry also repairs toys, bicycles, sewing machines—nearly anything that can be brought to the shop. He works rapidly at the jobs during the evening and weekends. Items that need parts are set aside after noting the parts needed on a "want list." Early the next morning before the shoppers are out, Harry's wife takes off for the city to pick up parts. Parts clerks recognize her time problem, so she gets speedy service at will-call counters.

When the Fix-It Shop volume builds up, Harry will need more time for repairs. His wife will conserve his bench time by taking in and delivering items and picking up parts. Trips to town every day cost less than maintaining a large inventory of parts. "Time is my most important item," Harry reports. "When you're in business for yourself every time-saving trick you can think of pays off."

● Custom catering commits the family a bit differently. Carol Coe started making *hors d'oeuvres* for weddings and parties in her kitchen, part time. Her husband delivered the party fixin's after his factory shift. Only a few months after Carol started *Custom Catering,* she and her husband were booked weeks ahead. They move in as a team at parties. She handles the buffet and cooking. He tends bar. Both pitch in to clean up afterward. In the meantime, he keeps his regular job during the day.

FOR MOONLIGHTING SUCCESS, PLAN FOR FAMILY COMMITMENTS

Too little time and too little money can strain family relations. Unless your family concurs with your ambitions and your planned operations, you're in trouble! Don't treat this potential problem lightly. Otherwise, you may win success and lose your family. Instead, adopt a positive plan that commits every family member.

Communicate with Your Wife (or Husband) and Children

Working at two jobs for "their benefit" isn't enough. Your

spouse and children must know and understand your objectives, problems, and how you and they stand to gain from your business. Get them working with you–not against you. Here's how–

    ● Hold regular family conferences. Outline your objectives–set up the problem of income and potential gain for the whole family to see. Children respond surprisingly to this treatment. They swell with a feeling of importance because you treat them like adults.

    ● Ask for understanding from the wife (or husband) and children when time is short–when lack of sleep may leave nerves jangled.

    ● Report on successes no matter how small. If a big sale or a completed milestone follows a period of intense activity, give everybody a break. Treat the family to an outing, even if it's only dinner out for an evening. When things go badly, report that too. But–keep everybody informed on a regular basis.

Keep Everyone Active

Family businesses are as old as farming, where everyone took their turn in the fields and at routine chores. Look for opportunities where your children can contribute actively to the business. Even an eight-year-old can lick stamps for sending out bills. Older children may type letters, replace stock, sweep the floor, or handle any of the myriad of unskilled jobs. *Craft Training Institute,* for example, packaged kits of materials for each lesson. Assembling the many parts into kits took hours, but teen-agers handled the tasks easily. Selling at a store after school, helping with building, and running errands pay dividends by conserving your already-short time.

Teach the Family Business Methods

Use the communication and part-time help plans for training as well as for building family spirit. Teach your spouse how to operate the business. Expose your children to business functions and the competitive environment. When you bring them in as part-time partners, they also learn from your mistakes. Such business know-how may benefit them more than the added income. Your children are motivated to become independent thinkers. You teach your family business methods by—

● Assigning them functions on a rotating basis. Let one of the teen-agers work with you in developing and operating an inventory system. Assign another to check the relative costs of making or buying parts. Ask your wife to learn tax and payroll accounting, (preferably during the planning stages). When you train more than one person to handle each function, one can substitute for another if the need arises.

● Brainstorm for ideas as a family. The technique of brainstorming is detailed in Chapter 2. Basically, you call on your spouse and children to help solve problems and develop new sales or production ideas.

● Give teen-agers responsibility quickly as they learn. No plan develops skills and maturity faster than assigned responsibility.

Try for Family Cohesiveness

Instead of letting time and money problems divide a family, turn them into a cohesive force. When money is being invested in the business instead of spent for fun, advise everyone that potential profits will come sooner if everyone pitches in. Turn your business problems into family problems and work them out as a group. Bring your family in—don't turn them out. Motivating wife or husband and children to help by assigning them real responsibilities cuts them in at every level. Sharing of responsibilities and problems builds cohesion in the family. Taking all the load yourself can be, and often is, a divisive force.

2

How to Find Your
Fortune-Building Opportunity

Look at problems as opportunities. Demands for services, applications of new technology, and extensions of existing products open endless opportunities for the astute entrepreneur. Look for business opportunities where you and your friends sense a need that offers a chance to turn your skills and know-how into cash. You can search most fruitfully where problems appear to be most intense, such as—

- *Turning waste products into a useful product or material.*
- *Providing fun and recreation for expanding populations.*
- *Combining engineering technology with medical needs in the expanding field of bioengineering.*
- *Sovling our horrendous environmental problems— removing or reducing air and water pollution, for a starter.*
- *Relieving the shortage of housing through new, low-cost remodeling or factory-built new housing.*
- *Satisfying the growing needs for personal security.*
- *Inventing new products or improving old ones.*
- *Reversing the "fill-a-need" routine to find jobs for existing capabilities—for profit.*

Businesses succeed because they serve a need. So, to find your business opportunity, find an unfilled need—and then fill it. Here's how—

First, look for *unfilled* needs—and many are noted in this chapter.

Second, look for needs being poorly filled—or filled inadequately.

Third, look for better ways to serve existing needs.

Learn to sniff out opportunities that others have overlooked. Newspapers and magazines chronicle new business ventures. Articles report how founders started a new business and are now successful, independent, and rich as a result. A number of real businesses are singled out in this chapter to highlight specific examples of how others have seized an idea and run with it. Don't expect to copy any of these ideas exactly, although you might adapt one of these ideas for your community. Instead, read and examine the techniques for finding a business opportunity. Learn how to open your eyes to potential needs to be filled—to sense opportunities for making your own personal fortune.

Later chapters spell out step-by-step procedures for setting up and operating a business according to type. Later chapters specify how to get help and how to handle specific problems. But, this chapter aims to broaden your horizons—to help you answer the questions, "Where and how can I find that idea for my own business—the idea that's 'just right' for me?" You need not look blindly. Problem areas, for example, signify unmet needs. Take junk cars, for example.

PROFITS FROM JUNKED CARS

Five million junked cars must be disposed of each year. At most junkyards, black smoke curls up as soft trim burns out. A big steel ball then bangs the bodies into smaller chunks for hauling to a steel mill. But, innovative handling increases the profits from junk.

Central Processing

The Sternoff Brothers in Seattle thought of a better way for turning cars into scrap. Their fragmentizer turns complete cars into finger-size pellets in 60 seconds. Thirty-four 300-pound hammers spin around a 20-ton rotor at 840 RPM in the fragmentizer to chew up bumpers, tough steel alloy axles, body sheet metal—everything. Friction develops 500-degree temperatures that quickly burn cloth, rubber, plastic, and oil. Fans cycle the smoke through a stack cleaner that removes chemicals and dirt—no more black smoke to pollute the air. Every couple of hours a rail-hopper car fills with the easily handled scrap that steel mills prefer.

Portable Processing

Allen Sharp and Jon Kneed also looked at the junked car problem and saw a potential for profit. They looked at the rusting junkers literally all over the landscape. But the scrap value wasn't worth long-distance hauling costs. Sharp and Kneed figured—"Let's process cars where we find them, rather than haul them to a central unit."

Combining their talents into a new company, Al-Jon, Inc., the two built a portable car-crusher. Huge jaws crush cars at a rate of 16 per hour. The end product is a metal "pancake" that can be stacked and hauled efficiently. When all the junkers at one location are converted into truckloads of scrap pancakes, the crusher moves on to the next highway eyesore. Result—waste becomes a useful product and our landscape is improved.

Chemical Processing

Still another method of disposing of junk autos was developed in Canada by the Peace River Mining & Smelting, Ltd. Instead of crushing the bodies for melting scrap, the Peace River operation dissolves them in hydrochloric acid. Treating the ferrous chloride solution produces high-purity iron sponge and powder. Huge presses form the iron powder directly into new automotive parts. The plant handles up to 2,000 scrap cars per day.

Salvaging Used Auto Parts

Nearly every town and all cities support used auto parts dealers—15,000 in the United States. These salvage artists rescue useable parts and assemblies from wrecked cars for resale to garages and repair shops. They not only reduce the number of junk cars, but save cost-conscious motorists bundles of cash for repairs.

Each of these companies took a different path to solve all or part of the same problem—

● Sternoff Brothers expanded their junk metal operations in steps until they could justify spending $1 million developing their unique but highly profitable fragmentizer. By starting small, building a step at a time, trying new ideas, producing useful products from waste, and keeping an eye always on profits, they built their own fortune from junk.

● Allen Sharp and Jon Kneed not only turned their unique idea into a profit, but they now offer portable and semiportable car-crushers for sale—so others can follow their example.

● Chemical processing of junk cars exemplifies the technical approach (See Chapter 5). You might set up a similar plant or simply find new uses for the iron powder product.

You can start looking for your fortune-building idea by brainstorming.

BRAINSTORMING FOR MONEY-WISE IDEAS

Money-wise ideas, like salvaging junk cars, are everywhere just waiting to be discovered. How do you find them? Try "Brainstorming." This technique stimulates imagination and creativity. The catchy term and the process are generally credited to Alex Osborn, a co-founder of the advertising firm of Batten, Barton, Durstine and Osborn. His book, _Applied Imagi-_

*nation** defines brainstorming techniques and tells you how to go about it. You can practice brainstorming through

● Developing your own creative abilities by tackling puzzles and think games. Creative writing, chess, fine arts, or drama also stretch your thinking. Just as regular exercise builds muscles and endurance, regular, forced thinking in creative, imaginative pursuits builds mind-power.

● Getting rid of your creative "cramps." Forget such ideas as "It won't work," or "Somebody has already thought of it." Plunge ahead boldly in your thinking.

● Writing ideas down when they occur to you. Once you get the feel of brainstorming, you'll find one idea tumbling after another through association, slanting of old ideas, and turning thoughts to new directions.

● Putting your subconscious mind to work. Writers, artists, designers—creative people in all media—understand the idea-ability of the subconscious. Feed your mind facts about problems, needs to be filled, capability waiting for something to do—all just before bedtime. Ideas will float to the surface of your mind the next day in what appear to be flashes of intuition.

● Channeling your creative thinking. Work on one specific problem at a time. Write down all thoughts as they occur to you. You can sort them out later as to practicality. One idea kicks off another. Combining parts of other ideas into still another follows the idea-association principle.

TURNING WASTE INTO PROFITS

Just a few examples of how creative thinking people have turned a minus (waste) into a plus (profit) are—

● Wood chips and mulch—Power and telephone companies, homeowners, and city crews remove trees and limbs to protect wires or homes. Instead of carting off the green trees and limbs to be burned, a shredder converts them to a mulch. The wood chips mixed

---

*Osborn, Alex F., *Applied Imagination,* Charles Scribner's Sons, New York, 1953.

with a high-nitrogen fertilizer are excellent for improving heavy soils. With a shredder, Alex B–makes $9,500 a year in his spare time turning a waste product into a profit. Every community needs this kind of service.

● Nut shells and fruit pits are ground to small bits for air blast polishing. Softer than sand blasting, the ground shells and pits remove grease and scale without damaging delicate surfaces. Your technical know-how and selling efforts can turn these ideas into your own profit producers.

● Scrap fish are processed into fish protein concentrates (FPC) as a low-cost source of protein supplement by Ocean Harvesters. Billions of pounds of fish not now being caught for food are available for conversion to relieve protein-deficient diets.

● Salvaging waste isn't limited to throw-aways. A roaring market was discovered for old computers. As IBM, Honeywell, Sperry-Rand, Burroughs, National Cash Register, and Control Data develop bigger, faster computers, older models are pushed aside. Like used cars, there's still plenty of mileage in used computers. One company, George S. Mc Laughlin Associates, Inc., leases or operates used computers and turned in $4 million of sales,with the business rapidly expanding. Used computers range in price down to 25 per cent of the new price.

New ideas for turning waste into something saleable are reported regularly in the *Wall Street Journal, Business Week,* and the financial section of your local newspaper.

FORTUNE OPPORTUNITIES IN RAPIDLY EXPANDING INDUSTRIES

Looking for potential business opportunities is much like fishing; you drop your line and lure where the fish are most likely to be.

Fun and Recreation Markets

Supply still lags behind demand in many recreational areas. Sporting goods sell at a $4 billion-a-year clip. Television sports coverage adds to the demand for everything from footballs for backyard "touch" games to new steel and aluminum tennis racket frames. But, you don't have to be Mr. Big in the business to cash in

● Robert L—designed and began making epoxy plastic ski boots. During the 1965-66 season, he sold 1,200 pairs. For promotion, he equipped the Olympic ski teams with free boots. The next year he sold 23,000 pairs and is doubling production each year—and the boots sell for up to $135 per pair.

● Custom Foam Fit Boots offer the skier perfect fit, warm feet, precise edge control—and total comfort. Two skiers, Ray Johnson and John Mulhollan, developed the process for pouring an expanding polyurethane foam between foot and boot. The process begins by stripping all padding and extraneous pieces out of oversize buckle boots. A nylon-lined skin diver sock slips over regular thermal ski socks on the skier's foot. With the sock-covered foot in the boot, expandable foam is injected behind the ankle. The boot is quickly buckled to hold in the expanding foam. In a few minutes, the foam sets chemically, and the foot can be pulled out—the foam lining perfectly fitted to one person's foot. The two innovators expect to license the custom-fitting process to ski shops all over the world.

● Skiing, the "in" winter sport for several years, is still growing wildly. Ski manufacturers and resort operators have made millions. Others, like the F.B. School of Seattle, Washington, earn up to $30,000 each season teaching novices and experienced skiers how to ski better. Land purchased for a pittance now sells for up to $80,000 an acre for condominiums or ski cabins near developed slopes. Development of new and better equipment from skis and boots to stylish wardrobes for the slopes and *apres-ski*, improved teaching methods and vacation packages, food and lodging near ski areas—all offer business opportunities bounded only by one's imagination and capital.

● Camping trailers, either the folding tent variety or the "tag-along" house types, are selling so fast the problem now is—where to spend the night? See Chapter 8—concerning franchises for ideas on how to cash in on travel trailers and campgrounds.

● Fish-and-game farms are another recreational growth opportunity. Pressures for hunting and fishing long ago exceeded the sustaining capacity of natural resources. So, more than 3,000 game farms raise ring-necked pheasants, quail, chukars, or other game birds for hunters to shoot all winter long—no season, no license. For example, the H—Game Farm 40 miles outside of Chicago raises pheasants in huge wire-topped pens. From November through February, they entertain hunters on weekends, provide dogs to help the hunters flush out the pheasants released into their wild, boggy lands around the house, and dress the bagged birds when hunters return home—all in one day. They charge $450 for a 30-bird card. Expensive? Not really when proximity and shooting results are considered. Actually, cost is seldom a consideration for H—Game Farm customers. Men who like the outdoors willingly pay almost any price for shooting privileges.

You can start your own private shooting preserve if you own or can lease wild land close to metropolitan centers. Find out more about this booming recreational business by first reading *Shooting Preserve Management—The Nilo System* by Dr. Edward L. Kozicky and John Madson (available from Conservation Department, Winchester ,Western Div., Olin Mathieson Co., East Alton, Illinois, 62024). The North American Game Breeders & Shooting Preserve Association sponsors an annual workshop for members and interested would-be members. Membership in the NAGB & SPA brings bulletins and aids for operation of association members.

● Fishermen are even more plentiful than hunters. Private fishing streams, ponds, and lakes (like the game farms) need not limit catches or seasons. Fishermen at the Cold Stream Park pay only for the fish they catch; for example, $1.80 per pound for rainbow trout cleaned and ready for the pan. State agencies license game farms and fish hatcheries. A game farm, for example, must release a fixed percentage of pheasants, quail, chukars, or doves. Hatcheries also raise game fish for private clubs or pond owners. The Johnson Fish Farm outside of Boulder, Colorado, originally raised rainbow trout for restaurants. Now, most of its keeper-size trout travel by tank truck for stocking private ponds and streams.

● Cold, clear water rushing from underground springs in Idaho provide ideal conditions for raising rainbow trout. But Idaho is a long way from the fancy restaurants and fish markets of Eastern cities. Air cargo now cuts distance to hours, and fresh trout arrive in Boston and Washington hours after being loaded into iced containers in Salt Lake City. One trout farm in Idaho now ships more than a million pounds of fresh trout to Eastern markets. Trout grow from hatching to about 13 inches and 10-12 ounces in 14 months. When a machine for deboning trout becomes available, pan-ready trout will fly daily from Idaho's clear-water ponds to city supermarkets.

● Summer camps are becoming big business. Camps of every variety, from bike tours through the national parks to dietary camps for fat teen-agers, are making money during the summer. Affluence is the key. Parents have the money and want their privacy—so junior and sis are off to camp when school is out. Whatever the reason, parents shell out from $800-$900 to as much as double that. Camping today is a $600 million industry. Short seasons jibe nicely with the availability of college students and teachers. You can start small with a camp, then expand every season.

● Boating is another sail-away business that's reaping profits for those who recognize an opportunity. Marinas for wet storage almost always have waiting lists. Selling boats, servicing engines and boats, sailing lessons for kids and women—the follow-on activities are almost endless. One enterprising innovator solved his problem of too little dolly storage space for ski boats and outboard runabouts by adapting a lift truck to hoist boats off dollies into vertical pigeon-holes three or four high. Boat trading is a game played faster and more furiously than car trading. And boat trading is almost always UP. An owner upgrades his 14-foot ski boat to a 16-foot model—at double the horsepower. The next move up is to a 20-foot cruiser—then a 26-foot cabin cruiser with head and galley. Beyond that are the live-aboard types that cost over $100,000. And there's always a novice ready to pick up the 14-footer at the bottom of the ladder. Refurbishing boats with college or high-school manual labor can be profitable for the profit-conscious marina operator, particularly during the off-season.

● Backpacking into remote wilderness areas is growing more popular as auto-accessible campgrounds become as crowded as Grand Central Station. The J&J Sport Company of Seattle built a new business on a scientifically designed pack frame. A patented connection permits fitting each bag to a wearer regardless of size for efficient load-carrying. Now the partners build packs for hikers plus special packs for guides and back-country prospectors. The key factor—a new and better pack invented to answer a known need.

● Renting big-ticket playthings to club members is the unique idea behind Recreation Fund. The Fund rents out cabin cruisers, sailboats, beach-front condominiums in Hawaii, motor homes, airplanes, and mountain cabins for about half the going rate. How can the Fund operate at half-price rates? This way: Fund members invest $1,000 each in a membership like a mutual fund. The Fund buys pleasure facilities, such as boats and cabins. Members obtain their dividends by using the club's facilities at cut rates. Members pay $5 a month dues. When they withdraw, $800 of their membership equity is returned. Members use a variety of facilities too costly for them to own alone. Also, "dividends" in using facilities are tax free.

Economics of Recreation Fund work out like this—A thousand members, each contributing $1,000 of capital, can own $1 million in facilities. Monthly dues gross $5,000. The rental fee for each facility, even at roughly half the going rate, fully pays for depreciation and maintenance. The user pays for any fuel burned. No limit is imposed on usage—the more members use the facilities, the greater their "dividends."

There's money to be made in the fun field. But good management is particularly needed. Too many operators are fun types first and managers second.

Bioengineering

Medicine and engineering, bioengineering, are working to: (1) control the spiraling cost of medical care, and (2) devise new methods and equipment for treating new and old ills. Magnetics, ultrasonics, bioluminescence, infrared, and radiation detection are improving diagnosis. Radioisotopes injected into a patient's blood and viewed through a gamma-ray imaging system that looks like a TV tube permit a doctor to trace blood flow through a patient. Similarly, iron-bearing materials can be manipulated through a patient. For instance, iron-bearing materials can be manipulated through the intestinal tract with magnets to improve X-ray examinations. Automatic blood sampling, pulse sensing, blood-pressure reading, etc., are fall-outs from research for the U.S. man-in-space projects. Kidney machines, artificial heart pacers, infrared thermal mapping in search of tumors, and radioisotope systems are all relatively recent developments. Each new development opens the way for a dozen more—and every one opens a business opportunity.

The search for new drugs has entered the ocean. Equipment now available speeds the tests for antibiotic activity. Better centrifuges aid antiviral research. The opportunities for the trained and imaginative inventor or innovator in the field of medicine, either for treatment or research, appear limitless. With Medicare and Medicaid extending treatment to millions who never had adequate care, the market is wide open.

Bioengineering developments require special knowledge and technical know-how. How you can start and operate a technically based business is detailed in Chapter 5. Opportunities noted here provide only a tempting glimpse of a field so wide open even the limits are unknown.

Steer Clear of Declining Industries

While opportunities may exist in railroading, mining, or public transit, the chances are slim compared to expanding areas such as oceanography (just leaving the shore), bioengineering, and recreation. If you are fishing for a business opportunity, drop your line and lure into new pools rather than old, fished-out streams.

SOLVING PROBLEMS—EARN A FORTUNE

Finding solutions to big problems can put millions in profits in your pockets. And, the world is flooded with big problems—like garbage disposal, air pollution, water management, substandard housing. The list is a long one—and grows longer rather than shorter each year. Let's look at a few problems and note how they can become your opportunity.

Waste Management

Disposing of garbage and the mountains of cardboard, bottles, cans, etc., poses an almost superhuman problem. Twenty years ago each of us threw away about 2 pounds of trash each day. Today, trash averages 7 1/2 pounds per person every day—that's 750,000 tons every day. And the rate is going up. By year 2,000, the average family will be throwing away twice as much garbage and trash as today. So—more trash per family and a growing number of families add up to a waste management crisis. No real answers are in sight, although some innovative approaches are being tried—

● A Japanese company is using a product-from-waste approach. First, garbage is compressed into dense, hard chunks. Next, machines wrap the dense chunks with a light wire mesh. The whole mess is then dipped in hot asphalt. Tests indicate that the garbage chunks so treated are hygienic, and do not shrink. Possible uses for the blocks—land reclamation, roadbeds—even houses.

● Garbage, as distinct from refuse and trash, has been successfully composted and converted into a soil-improving humus.

● A West Coast inventor developed a machine that reduces collected rubbish to one-tenth its normal volume so land-fill sites can hold ten times as much trash. Innovation in handling trash is already changing the whole system, and the opportunities are just beginning to open.

● Collection of garbage and trash is becoming a problem as big as disposing of the stuff once it's collected. Who can forget the sanitary workers' strikes? Garbage piled up in streets, and clothespins on the nose were the fashion of the day. One innovative answer for collecting trash is to dump it into pipelines and blow or wash it to a disposal site. Pilot projects in Europe are already moving refuse by pneumatic pipeline from huge apartment complexes to a central incinerator. Garbage disposals in homes grind food scraps and wash remains down the sewer. Professor Iraj Zandi at the University of Pennsylvania has studied the feasibility of grinding bottles, cans, and other trash and garbage into small bits, mixing the stuff with water, and flushing it all away in pipelines.

Air and Water Pollution

Like the birds who foul their own nests, humanity is rapidly turning city air into smoky, eye-watering smog, lakes and rivers into open cesspools, and ocean beaches into hazardous, ugly disaster areas. A whole new frontier of opportunities awaits you, as the innovative entrepreneur, to sweep back the tide of pollution from air and water. Antipollution laws can provide the incentive, but only imaginative development can provide answers. Some of the potentials include—

● Auto exhaust cleanup—Some system to stop the millions of tons of wastes being discharged into our air must be developed—and soon. Millions await the developers of the bright ideas that effectively reduce auto exhaust emission.

● Biological treatment of industrial wastes may be the key for clearing up streams and lakes. Research has turned up insects that biologically control harmful insects—so fewer chemical insecticides are needed. The developers of practical systems for controlling pollution can write their own ticket.

● Stack cleaners already remove tons of chemicals and solids from factory smokestacks—but much remains to be done. What is needed are more effective, less costly scrubbers. Economics and the law are both factors in this game of "let's clean up the air." New ideas and equipment have a wide-open field.

● Thermal pollution is a new threat. Nuclear power plants are quiet, clean, and enormously efficient. But, they generate a new kind of waste heat. Heat transferred to rivers raises water temperatures enough to disrupt the ecology of streams. Instead of a waste, consider nuclear heat as a resource. Finding a practical use for this waste heat could be your key to a fortune.

Housing

Dilapidated, crowded housing leads to crime and other city problems. Yet, housing costs are skyrocketing. Tearing down and rebuilding or remodeling offer partial solutions. *Operation Breakthrough* sponsored by the Department of Housing and Urban Development (HUD) is taking giant steps. Opportunities for turning these problems into cash include—

● Remodeling with new materials to beat the cost squeeze in some cities. Packaged bathrooms, easily handled plastic piping, lightweight structural beam assemblies, and new wall systems permit quick refurbishment of heavy brick and stone structures. As a result, posh apartments replace blight. As a builder with low overhead and a nose for profits, you could profitably remodel many existing buildings—better, actually than big, inflexible operators.

● Borrowing ideas from the trailer manufacturers to produce homes on assembly lines. Resistance from unions and restrictive building codes are crumbling before the economic advantages of building housing inside factories, away from the weather. Big pieces, housing halves, or whole apartment units complete with carpeting on the floor, are being hauled to prepared sites and quickly erected.

● Building components for small builders. Multi-unit complexes house families at less cost for land. Your opportunity—build new areas with inviting open space and community recreation areas using low-cost components, or manufacture the components for builders.

Broad Range Problems

You don't have to be a systems manager or organize a big company to profit from problem-oriented opportunities. Individuals and small businessmen can cash in by solving parts of problems. For example—

● Devices that promote personal safety and security open possibilities as crime increases. An ultrasonic burglar alarm fills a room with sound waves too high to hear. Any movement sets off an alarm. The unit is so simple it plugs into a wall outlet and sells by mail. Alarm systems for cars, chemical weapons to protect the pedestrian at night, new locking systems to keep intruders out—all are open opportunities for you to profit from.

● Sewage, salt water, fume stacks, and piping are tough on metal tanks. So, New-Chem Tanks, Inc., takes the direct approach and builds tanks that avoid metal corrosion by eliminating the metal. The innovator borrowed a technique devised originally for building rocket cases—winding glass fibers around a form and encasing the fibers in corrosion-resistant plastic. Tanks and piping are lightweight, stronger than steel, and limited in size only by shipping facilities.

● Corrosion on a smaller scale builds a business for an engineer who sells small magnesium anodes to protect automotive radiators. The magnesium anodes control corrosion by neutralizing the acids. Another company sells sump drain plugs for oil, transmission, and differential cases equipped with powerful magnets to attract and hold metal chips.

● Parking lots in downtown areas use cleared ground for parking until plans are ready for building. But, one layer of cars can't use high-cost land efficiently. Yet, building a multi-story lot for one or two years' use hardly pays off. So, Portable Parking Structures builds three-layer parking garages on temporary leases from prefabbed steel and precast concrete slabs. The portable structures can be set up or taken down within a week. Simple? Of course, but the company grossed $7 million in one year and is growing fast.

● Problems not solved include some real head-scratchers. For example, how can manufacturers distribute their do-it-yourself (DIY) products for the home? Hardware stores don't have the space and clerks don't have the know-how to counsel homeowners. Homeowners would buy them if they knew about them and could use the new products. You might consider a demonstration-party-get-together system to distribute such products. Or sponsor in-store demonstrations of products, tools, and materials specifically designed for DIY maintenance.

Problems can be turned into business opportunities. Your job, create the right combination of utility, costs, logistics, and price to turn problems into profits.

MAKE YOUR FORTUNE FROM
BETTER PRODUCTS AND SERVICES

Like Gresham's law of money—good products drive out the bad. Change is a way of life—and the pace is quickening. New products, new ways of doing old jobs, lower-cost products that do the same job—all are finding a market and lining the pockets of astute businessmen, big and small. Even if this book were several volumes thick, it couldn't list all the new and better products that are finding markets today. But just a few examples indicate how imaginative businessmen and inventors are finding new ways to build profits, and you can take your cue from their success—

● STP, an oil-additive marketed by Andy Granatelli, has become a national symbol—kids plaster stickers on everything from homemade racers to school notebooks—and STP sells close to $40 million worth of products a year.

● Solid-state electronics and a car's 12-volt electrical system combine to provide up to 20 amperes of power. Converters operate electrically powered tools at vacation sites or for small builders. A simple box replaces a complete motor-generator set at one-quarter to one-third the price.

● Fireplaces provide nostalgic moments for fire-watchers, but the old-fashioned masonry units add $1,000 or more to a house. Freestanding metal units with insulated stacks go in for one-third the price—and they burn fewer, smaller logs.

● Convenience foods, the kind you heat and serve, are appearing in endless variety. Processing costs add to the cost-of-living index, but, time is money to the working housewife. So, big and small businesses are cashing in. You don't have to be a national marketer to produce and sell convenience foods in local markets.

● New tools which work better and faster compensate for lack of skills. Demand from do-it-yourselfers grows as the "fix-it" handyman disappears.

● Touching up the nicks on your car's exterior paint is now easier, thanks to a handy tube and applicator of a new solid (90 per cent) compound formulated to match auto manufacturers' exact production colors. The touch-up compound dries quickly to a glossy finish without rubbing. Forest Interiors Corp. makes the touch-up kits which are distributed through the auto manufacturers' own parts system. Another product is a waxy crayon of colored materials for filling in nail holes after installing prefinished wood paneling. Forest Interiors now does a multimillion dollar business that started when Jack Leutzinger first boiled up a pot of pigmented wax and paste on his wife's kitchen stove to make *Putty Stik.*

YOUR FORTUNE POTENTIAL— FINDING JOBS FOR CAPABILITY

Lining up jobs for available talent reverses the axiom "Find a need and fill it." Instead, you recognize a capability or resource and find a job for it. College students, for example, offer an almost unlimited labor resource. But, they can work only part time on odd schedules. Your profit opportunity—find jobs that fit students' schedules.

Putting Students to Work

According to the Labor Department, 8.2 million students, ages 16 to 24 held jobs during one year. Two-thirds of those students worked at jobs less than 35 hours per week and earned an average of $900 per year. Yet, more students look for than find jobs. Successful businesses based on using student manpower include—

● Dean's Student Service operated at a major university in a suburb. Dean, a student in the graduate business school, operated the service while going to school himself—and grossed between $8,000 and $9,000 a year—mostly profit. Essentially, he operated an employment service. Homes in the vicinity regularly hired part-time help for raking leaves, putting up or taking down storm windows, cleaning a basement, painting, lawn mowing and maintenance, and other jobs too numerous to mention.

Dean advertised in the local paper. Results were great for everyone—Dean paid his way through college; students earned part of their expenses ; customers had access to a reliable part-time service. See Chapter 3 for details on how you can start a similar student service in your locality.

● Key-punch operations use part-time students during evening hours, usually on a four-hour shift.

● Mail-order handling uses part-time student help. Such activities are labor intensive; that is, they call for little capital and much individual handling. Students open envelopes, record transactions, pick orders from stock, and wrap them for shipment.

● Generally student manpower offers a number of advantages—

—Lower rate per hour to start,with increases keyed to reliability and time availability.

—High motivation—students need the work and are usually grateful to employers who make work available on a schedule compatible with school classes.

—Little interest in unionization, fringe benefits, or advancement to management positions.

—Tremendous resources in terms of man-hours available.

Students present problems too :

—Their primary interest is school, not their job. So,

exams take precedence. Studies sometimes interfere with work schedules.

  —Vacations break up continuity during summer, on holidays, and between school terms.

  —Not all students are reliable and schedule conscious.

Despite the continuing migration to the cities, many people prefer semi-rural environments even if jobs are scarce. You can tap these labor pools profitably—often with the active aid of local businessmen. Taking a business into a labor-rich area can solve a number of problems for small businessmen—

 ● Local businessmen may supply money either by subscription of stock or loans from the area's banks.

 ● Rent-free facilities during start-up activities. Sometimes, a special building may be constructed as part of an agreement to move in a business that generates jobs.

 ● Willing workers who appreciate an opportunity to work near their home instead of having to pull up stakes and move to a city.

 ● Lack of competition for a limited supply of skilled workers.

 ● Active state-sponsored programs to train new workers.

Typical of the advantages derived from moving a business is J & J Jackets. The owner moved production of sports jackets out of a labor-short city area to a town 80 miles away. There, the main business was logging and fishing—both highly seasonal and subject to wide-swinging fluctuations. Almost no opportunities existed for wives to work. In the city, J & J's production manager had to compete for the few trained power-machine operators available with higher pay. The town, on the other hand, offered a large building rent-free plus help in recruiting trainees. The state cooperated by training workers specifically for the power-machine jobs. Start-up costs were high because the workers were slow at first. But, they got better. Overall, the move was a good one—reduced unit costs for jackets and jobs for people without work opportunities.

Happy Housewives Labor Pool

Despite the more than 15 million working wives, millions

more feel trapped in the house or apartment and have a yen to make extra money. You can tap this labor pool with imagination, patience, and the ability to operate with skinny profit margins. Typical of the operating firms tapping this resource are—

- Overload services that supply skilled help for short-time jobs. Kelly Girl, Manpower, Inc., and Office Overload are typical firms that put housewives to work two or three days a week or for two- or three-week intervals. Usually, these employees prefer part-time work because of family responsibilities or other interests. The housewives are skilled secretaries, keypunch operators, or clerks. They worked full time before their marriage, so they require little more than brush-up training. National franchises advertise these services, along with small local firms.

- A correspondence school bundles up its work and delivers it to skilled housewives who work in their own home while tending to their small children. Pay is on a unit basis, so the women work on their own schedule.

- Typing is a key element for another mail-order operator. He puts letters and other typing on tape and delivers it, with a portable transcriber unit, to homes. There, former secretaries pound away on their own typewriters at so much per page. Combination dictating-transcribing tape units now cost only about $30-$60. They last for years, and the reuseable tape cassettes neatly package work assignments. Housewives furnish their own typewriter and work at home. Overhead for the company is mainly a student with a car for delivery and pickup, plus the investment in dictating-transcribing units.

3

How to Become Independent
in Your Own Service Business

Are you dissatisfied with the quality of services you pay high prices for? Then you know about the opportunities in fixing TV's, automotive service stations, auto repairs, restaurants, plus the many other personal services we all depend on. Costs of services are skyrocketing, but look at the other side. Rising prices boost your chances for profits in your own service business. You can start your service business by—

- *Opening and operating your own automotive service station that can build a business paying up to $40,000 or more for a single station.*
- *Following step-by-step the route to a multiple service station business.*
- *Repairing cars for a profit under the price umbrella of the big new-car repair shops and their costly overhead.*
- *Serving delicious food in a style people enjoy.*
- *Combining your service skills with sales for double profits in many fields from tailoring to appliance "fix-it" shops.*

Dissatisfied with the service you get and the price you pay for it? These facts point up the opportunities for you to earn your fortune in one of the service businesses—

● Services of all kinds account for more than half (51.6 per cent) of the United States' Gross National Product.

● Prices for services are rising faster than any other major part of the Consumers Price Index. When the CPI for all items was up 24 per cent and food was up 22 per cent, the cost of services was up 36 per cent. And the cost of services is still rising.

● Small businessmen supply most services except for government ones. Opportunities are wide open in practically every service activity you can name.

● Service-oriented businesses are labor intensive, require relatively little capital to start, and depend mainly on the ability of the owner-operator.

BIG-MONEY OPPORTUNITIES IN AUTOMOTIVE SERVICES

Automobiles play such a big part in our lives, you have to consider all the services connected with cars first—from gasoline stations to specialized repair shops.

Service Stations

Close to 225,000 service stations offer gasoline, lubricating oil, and car necessities in the U.S. Outstanding station operators earn up to $50,000 per year. Many make from $20,000 to $30,000. But, turnover is high. About one-fourth of the independent operators move on to something else in a typical year. If there's big money to be made in the service station business, how do the successful ones do it?

Let's look at Bud's Richfield. First, the station is located in a suburban district. Bud concentrates on repairs and repetitive maintenance oil changes, lubrications, brakes, exhaust systems, tune-ups—and gasoline sales. Bud's "I-want-to-help" attitude and down-to-earth approach have built a loyal following among the area's residents. Demand for his services keeps him so busy he books repair jobs two to three weeks ahead. Gasoline sales run 80,000 to 100,000 gallons per month—a high-volume station by industry standards.

The business obviously pays Bud well. He drives a new Cadillac, takes vacations totaling about six weeks a year, and lives in a $50,000 home. He also works long hours—but never on Sunday. Key factors that make Bud's Richfield station so profitable—

- Bud is personally available to customers. He "runs" his station and projects an image of genuinely wanting to be of help.
- He runs an honest shop and performs good work at fair prices. When a customer brings a car in for brake linings, he may replace only the front-wheel shoes because they wear so much faster. And the cost is approximately cut in half. Bud uses only long-life linings and insists on rebuilding or replacing wheel cylinders in the interests of safety. Bud says, "My customers are my friends. I wouldn't want my family driving in a car with worn or leaky brake cylinders, and I won't cut corners on my friends' cars. If a customer wants a cheapy job, he has to go somewhere else."
- Watching Bud and his crew work on a job is a pleasure, because they waste no motions. Productivity is high because they are trying to keep up with business rather than stretch jobs to boost prices. The crew beats flat-rate times on at least 95 per cent of their jobs.
- Word-of-mouth advertising attracts new customers. And, satisfied customers keep coming back in a steady stream—so no money goes out for gimmicks, special deals, games, or stamps—just good, friendly service at fair prices—not low, not high—but fair. Bud tells a story that sums up his business approach—"Remember the 'dumb' kid who always picked the nickel instead of the dime when asked to choose between the two coins? A do-gooder finally asked the boy 'Don't you know the dime is worth twice as much as the nickel, even if it is smaller? The 'dumb' kid replied, 'Sure, but if I pick the dime, nobody asks me again'." Bud states flatly, "I make it on repeat business."
- Bud hires high school and college students to handle routine jobs at low cost. As students learn, he breaks them in on oil changes and lubrication, teaches them about brake jobs and tune-ups. This

leaves his time free for emergencies and trouble-shooting. During the busy summer traveling season, students work all day. When schools are in session, Bud adjusts his own work schedule for more evening hours. Students work from about 3 p.m. to closing at 9 p.m. with different students alternating days. Saturdays are big days with a full student crew.

● Bud's service extends to house calls. He frequently takes off in his old pickup to get a balky car started, to change a tire that has gone flat in a garage, or to haul gasoline to a car that has run out. House-call service seldom pays for the time expended, but the service attracts new customers and keeps old ones coming back again and again. On the go the full day, Bud is never too busy to weld a broken wagon for a customer's boy or fix a flat on a bicycle.

● Record keeping is fast and accurate. Bud's wife handles that angle of the business. She keeps daily records of gas and oil sales, and bills regular customers for repairs. An accounting service, specializing in gasoline stations, compares ratios with industry standards to guide operations. Ordinarily, sales run about 70 per cent for gasoline, 4 per cent for oil and lubricants, 16 per cent for tires, batteries, and accessories (TBA), and 10 per cent for lubrication and labor. Bud typically runs a higher than average percentage for repairs.

Major oil companies build stations and lease them to individual operators. Although independents may own their own stations, about three-fourths of the stations belong to major oil companies. You need about $6,000 to $10,000 of your own money to start operating a station—some of which may be borrowed. Mainly, you need cash to buy the inventory of gasoline, tires, oil, and lubricants.

Surprisingly enough, greasy-thumb mechanics no longer qualify as prime candidates for operating service stations. A high-volume station may gross from $300,000 to $500,000 per year and employ 7 to 18 people. Management skills become more important than specific car know-how for keeping operations profitable. Take one accountant for example. He moved out of a West Coast community because smog bothered his daughter's asthma. Rather than take another accountant's job, he applied for a station lease. Shell sent him to school for four weeks. Before that, he had done little more than change a flat on his own car. Today, his Shell station nets the accountant more than $30,000 per year. The Regional Manager says—"The key difference was the accountant's managerial skill. He ran a balanced station—and most of all, provided good service."

YOUR STEP-BY-STEP GUIDE TO A BIG-MONEY SERVICE STATION

Oil companies look constantly for good men to operate their stations. Service stations constitute one of the biggest and oldest franchise operations in the United States today. Until you prove yourself, you may start at a small (under 20,000 gallons of gasoline per month) station. When you prove you can operate a small station, you move to a medium station (up to 60,000 gallons per month). Finally, you may move to a high-volume station—and real money. Take these steps in turn—

Learn the Business

Work for a successful service station operator, like Bud, for a few months to gain experience. Pick up time and cost-saving tips to improve service at a profit. Attend vocational school, at night if necessary, to learn automotive trouble-shooting, power mechanics, and how to use tools. Take on an evening shift at a station while retaining your present job, to gain experience and find out if you like the service station business.

Start Only When You're Ready

Make sure you acquire enough cash to see you through the start-up period. Own your tools outright. If possible, accumulate enough cash to buy the opening inventory without borrowing. Develop your own plan for financing (see Chapter 10), time management, marketing, and selecting employees.

Until you fully understand these functions, you're not ready to start.

Research the Field Thoroughly

Look specifically at these points—

 • Compare lease contracts offered by at least five oil companies. Look for differences in financing terms, technical and marketing assistance, customer credit provisions, station rental (minimum fee plus percentage of gross or net),training, insurance (business and personal), and station modernization plans. Your best bet—get sample copies of leases, lay them out on the floor, and compare each clause across the group. Look for additions in one, omissions from another, and varying percentages in all areas. Here's where you first exercise your analytical, managerial know-how. If you don't understand the legalese of an agreement, ask questions— you'll be amazed at how much information you get from asking "stupid" questions.

 • Study locations available—Does a station depend mainly on tourist traffic along a major highway, or is the station neighborhood oriented, like Bud's? Can customers leave a car for work while they shop, catch a bus to work, or attend a community college, high school, or special entertainment event? Location is mighty important, so check out every possibility and compare good points and weak points of each.

 • Check competition—Stations frequently appear in bunches, so find out BEFORE you sign a lease—How good is the service at competing stations? Are other stations national dealers or cut-rate locals or independents? How much business do they do? Check volume by counting cars, noting how many flow through the back shop for lubes and oil changes. You can do this by parking a short distance away and observing every in-and-out movement for several days, including weekends. You'll be surprised at how volume varies between two stations across the street from each other. Become a "customer" of a high-volume station to see what that station offers. Most likely you can sense immediately the difference between two competing stations. Your customers will sense that difference too, so make sure you project a "come-back-and-see-us" approach.

After Signing Your Lease

Follow these volume-building hints from successful service station operators—

● Key on providing fast, friendly service—Clean windshields immediately. Check the oil, look after tires, note cooling system and battery condition—and do it all with a smile—even if the customer is grouchy. Analyze how you like to be treated, and provide that kind of service to your customers. Satisfied customers come back again.

● Keep your station and yourself neat—Keep rest rooms spotlessly clean. Adopt a policy of wearing freshly laundered shirts and pants every day. Wipe up oil or grease spots to make sure customers don't pick up oily dirt on their shoes and transfer it to carpets at home. Cover seats with a cloth to prevent oil, grease, or dirt on your clothes from rubbing off on upholstery.

● Maintain a record system that provides you with answers— You need up-to-the-minute information on costs, sales, and earnings. If accounting is not your bag, ask your wife or a moonlighting accountant to help. You can't operate a business efficiently without good records—so, don't try.

● Get all the help you can from the oil company—Ask your company to sponsor a "Grand Opening" or "New Management" promotion when you take over. Use the company's full range of credit services, including its credit card plans for purchasing tires, batteries, and repairs. Take full advantage of any training classes or schools offered.

● Keep up to date—Check new-car service manuals for information on maintaining the new cars. Study trade magazines for tips and shortcuts. Pick the brains of suppliers for new ideas, materials, and systems and use that information to improve your service.

● Select employees for their honesty and motivation—Young workers, if motivated by the need for cash to attend school, or experienced adults who know how to work, can make the difference between a handful of personnel headaches and a smoothly operating station. Continuously counsel your employees to extend your own courteous, friendly attitude toward customers. Develop a rapport with your employees that will motivate them with your objectives—a profitable, smooth-running, service-oriented station.

● Manage your station. Don't just operate your station. Attend to—

—Marketing. Use coupons to build volume when starting up. Advertise winterizing or spring check-out specials. Offer "house-call" service in local shopping papers or telephone directories. Your station service trade magazines offer all kinds of volume-building ideas.

—Cost control. Watch for theft. Check on employee productivity by establishing times for lube and oil changes, establish manning schedules to match customer volume, and figure profitability of added services.

—Ratio analysis. Oil companies supply operating statistics and you can use them to study your own station's operation. Departure from norms can signify trouble ahead or added profitability.

—Employee relations. Picking the right workers, motivating them to put out top performance by your own example, on-the-job training, incentives and bonuses, and firm control by setting objectives and checking performance against those objectives—all are critical management actions.

HOW TO STEP INTO THE
BIG-TIME SERVICE BUSINESS

For really big money, manage more than one station or build up a station and sell out the volume operation and goodwill for capital gain. Learn how from these two smart operators—

● Claude Vacielly built a local chain of stations and sold out to an oil company to capitalize his profits. He started by leasing a single station from a major oil company. He built the station's volume quickly with top service. With a profitable performance record, he sold his lease. Using that capital, Claude built his own station on leased land, borrowing the difference (SEM, see Chapter 10). The investment was a big one, but he paid off the loans ahead of time. In steps he added seven more stations. His volume-building trick was to give out coupons with gasoline purchases that could be exchanged for lubrication, an oil change, or a wash. These jobs were done during slack periods. Coupon credits applicable on tires and batteries locked in customers and allowed Claude to retain his profits on tires and accessories while building gasoline volume. Coupon credits cost him less than price-cutting to meet competition head-on. He had built his string to eight stations before selling out to his oil company supplier. Claude's take, $40,000—taxed as a capital gain.

● Randy McGeorge built his chain of service stations with oil company money. He kept an eye out for failing stations that could be profitable. When he found one, Randy would take over the lease. Within a few months, the station would be doing up to three times its former volume. Randy really understood the pulling power of full customer service. But, Randy's ability to pick good people pays the biggest dividends. When an employee proves his worth, Randy brings him in as a limited partner and turns over control of a station to the new partner. Randy retains the lease, owns the inventory and equipment, and takes the major share of operating profits. The operating partner earns a percentage of the profits in addition to his salary. Randy provides centralized accounting service, management counsel, and financial backing. By adding stations to his chain and manning them with profit-motivated managers, Randy's income tops $100,000 a year—much more than he could earn running even the best single station.

HOW TO EARN YOUR FORTUNE
IN AUTO REPAIRS

Dissatisfaction with automotive repair services long ago topped the crisis level. Complaints from every corner of the country are aired in Congressional hearings. So, you know the opportunities are everywhere. Instead of working as a mechanic for a new car dealer, consider operating your own business. Putting your expertise to work in your own shop opens two opportunities for increasing your income: (1) you earn more per hour than you are paid as an hourly mechanic because you work faster, more productively; (2) you earn a profit on the parts you buy at wholesale prices and bill out at retail.

Here's how you can earn profits plus wages in your own business—

● Operate your repair shop along with a service station. Bud's

Richfield follows this pattern. The station lease provides space, a pneumatic hoist, and parking spaces around the building. Materials, such as oil, grease, and gasoline, are readily accessible. In Bud's case, gasoline and oil sales more than cover his overhead for facilities. Repairs generate his healthy profits.

● Rent low-cost space. Morgan's Auto Rebuild, for example, operates in an old store building abandoned in favor of a new· shopping center. Charlie Morgan caters specifically to insurance claims adjusters. He refuses to kite estimates to cover customers' deductibles, and his lower prices reflect his honesty. So, adjusters insist that clients get a bid from Morgan. His prices are sheltered under the umbrella of new-car dealer and big rebuild garage pricing schedules with their whopping overhead. Charlie offers pickup and delivery service—and his work is tops. Customers may grumble about not covering part of their deductible, but they come back for service on their own because his prices are honest.

● Ted S—built his auto repair business while attending college. He operated in a one-stall rented garage and worked only on professors' cars evenings and weekends. When Ted graduated, three students continued the operation. Ted continued to manage the business, supplying capital and know-how along with many weekend hours of his own under hoods to keep up with the business volume. Now, Ted is expanding the business again to make evening and weekend service available outside the university. Like the tail wagging the dog, Ted now finds managing and developing his own business more challenging and rewarding than his routine engineering job. His next step—operating the business full time. Beyond that, his plans call for franchising the idea to other university areas.

● Tips and hints you can use to earn more profits in your automobile repair business include—

   —Controlling overhead by stocking a minimum of parts. Buy parts from big suppliers who deliver as parts are needed. Cost of carrying parts, ordering to replace usage, space charges, and losses from theft more than balance the higher cost of parts delivered on short notice.

   —Hiring a professional accountant to keep records, determine which jobs return a profit and which are losers, advise on cash position, and handle tax accounting.

   —Buying and using as much cost-effective equipment

as possible. Diagnosis by electronics saves hours of cut-and-try methods. Pneumatic tire tools, nut runners, and power chisels save valuable hours. But, make a trial run to see if promised savings actually accrue before buying machines.

—Picking brains of suppliers for new materials and methods. Read trade magazines to pick up customer-satisfying and cost-cutting tips. Check consumer magazines too, like *Popular Mechanics,* for service and time-saving ideas.

—Selecting and training employees for productivity. Allow workers to earn a bonus for beating mutually acceptable time standards. By paying more, you get your pick of mechanics who are willing to work to earn more than bare minimum rates.

LEARN HOW FOOD SERVICES CAN BUILD YOUR FORTUNE

Restaurants open and close like books in study hall. Fast-food franchises are available from at least 240 different companies, some of them giants, like Kentucky Fried Chicken with 2,500 units and still growing. (See Chapter 8 with full details on acquiring and operating a franchise.) During 1969, Americans spent more than $25 billion on food in restaurants. By 1975, restaurants are expected to gross more than $50 billion per year—a healthy, growing market to shoot at despite competition.

Fine Restaurants

Edna's is a prime example of turning every minus into a plus. The first handicap is the name *Edna's.* Sounds like a quick-order joint, but *Edna's* became a "Celebrity Center." *Edna's* is located in a blighted, black slum area completely away from other businesses. But, there's plenty of parking available, and the area furnishes ample help for kitchen and dining room.

Although the building was old, imaginative lighting, a refurbished entrance, and a new interior provided a quietly plush backdrop for *Edna's* unique personality—at a fraction of the cost of a new building. She greeted customers herself and treated them like visiting royalty—remembering names, relating incidents, and chatting with apparent aimlessness. But, every word became grist for her "Celebrity Center" column—a unique advertisement that appeared weekly. She named names, noted parties, commented on "who was seen with whom" in a witty matrix that proved "must reading" for local townspeople. As her fame spread, out-of-towners took notice until *Edna's* became truly world famous.

Edna built her success on good food, basically, despite the publicity hoopla. She featured simple fare, real Italian spaghetti, chicken with exquisite sauces, and a variety of French cuisine that turned inexpensive beef and veal into gourmet dishes. She stayed clear of the brute approach—a hunk of raw beef broiled and served with a baked potato and green salad. In addition to serving dinners, Edna packaged her spaghetti sauce in cartons and froze it for marketing through a department store chain. Later she quick-froze other dinner favorites. These delicacies carried the *Edna's* label and a price tag with authority. One business complemented the other. The frozen food line was Edna's way of expanding rather than opening other restaurants.

Here's How to Make It BIG in Your Own Restaurant Business

● DINING out is not *eating* out—there's a difference, and the difference hinges on food quality and appearance. Learn to dress up the taste and look of food. Learn both by getting top training at either the American Culinary Federation, Work Study Program, Educational Institute of AH&MA, 221 West 57th Street, New York, N.Y. 10019 or the Culinary Institute of America, 393 Prospect Street, New Haven, Conn. 06511. You may also pick up training at local vocational schools or on the job in a fine restaurant. But expertise level varies greatly according to instructors.

● Pick your specialty—No restaurant can serve truck drivers at one door, supply teen-agers with hamburger-and-french-fry appetites at another, and maintain a dining room with plush atmosphere in front. Whether in a fast-food outlet or a fine restaurant, aim for a specific slot—don't try to cover everything.

● Know about food yourself—Don't depend on hiring a chef; good ones are too scarce. You supply the key ingredient, a thorough knowledge of every culinary art from buying to serving.

● Gain experience by working in a successful restaurant—If you aspire to operate a fine restaurant, work in one of the moving-up restaurants—not one that is coasting on its reputation. Learn about pastries, salads, be the *garde-manger* in charge of hot and cold *hors d'oeuvres,* prepare those delicious sauces as the *saucier* yourself, carve roasts, fowl, and fish as the *rotisseur,* and learn the tricks of where and how to buy for quality at everyday, low prices.

● Become creative by brainstorming (see Chapter 2)—Restaurants prosper by offering something different—unusual atmosphere, publicity like *Edna's,* entertainment that offers a change, or by catering to a specific slice of the populace—like *Sardi's* to theatergoers or the *Brown Derby* to moviemakers.

● But, don't lose sight of food, no creativity, atmosphere, or hoopla will compensate for substandard food. Restaurants are in business to serve food, and customer palates are learning to distinguish between so-so food and gourmet fare. Many little services build repeat business.

● Breads and home-flavored jams or jellies add an extra touch at little cost. Instead of hard, cold rolls, serve hot biscuits with honey, a warm "little loaf" on its own cutting board with a slicing knife for do-it-yourself action, or breadsticks to nibble on.

● Nibblings trays filled with low-cost pickles, beets, celery, a few olives, corn, relish, chives cottage cheese, and other goodies specialty of the house add a big plus to a meal with little cost.

● Tossing specialty salads on a cart right at the table lets customers see how ingredients are mixed and impresses patrons with the professionalism of the waitress or waiter. Mixing salads becomes part of your "show" or staging.

● Survey the many fine restaurants in your area and note those little touches that add to atmosphere, complement food, and contribute to your "good feeling." Note, too, those irritants that could keep you from returning—and strive to eliminate them from your own place. Irritants may come from an overly snobbish *maitre d'*,curt waitresses or waiters, slow service, cold food, big menus with only a limited number of items available, and many more.

● Learn to sense customer satisfaction or dissatisfaction. Talk at random with patrons as the host like Edna, learn regulars' names, spend enough time to really know your customers.

● Plan food and prices with one eye on the accounting sheet. Work with your accountant to check profit margins and other ratios against industry standards.

HOW TO DOUBLE-TEAM YOUR SERVICE SKILLS INTO PROFITS

Service skills can start you in business whether you are a TV repairman, a tailor, or other skilled serviceman. Learn to combine service with selling for a double payoff. Custom service plus a profit from goods sold can double or triple your current earnings. You stand to gain more by starting your own business based on your know-how than by continuing to work for someone else. All you need, if you are a skilled serviceman, is a system of selling your skills—like these examples—

Custom Tailoring

Benny G—pressed pants and fitted suits in a department store men's shop. He sewed cuffs on pants, altered shoulder lines, changed sleeve lengths on jackets, fixed loose seams or resewed loose buttons and, when these chores were finished, pressed a new garment for delivery. Benny earned wages for the custom work, the salesman pocketed the commission, and the store toted up the profit. But Benny figured he provided the key service element. So, he established his *Hong Kong Tailors*—a shop that sells suits, sports jackets, and slacks custom-tailored in Hong Kong from top-grade English woolens and European silk blends. Price is a key factor in Benny's marketing program. Suits sell for $65—and compare in quality with suits sold a few blocks away for $119.50 and up. Benny sells a suit custom-tailored for the same price as a ready-made suit from his plain racks—the only difference—a wait of about two months. You can adapt these proven money-making ideas from Benny's success plan—

- Don't advertise directly. Word-of-mouth spreads the news reliably if service and prices are "right."
- Operate from a shop on an upper floor of a downtown office building to keep overhead low.
- Offer top-quality materials plus the hand finishing Hong Kong tailors pride themselves on. As one satisfied customer tells another, volume builds steadily. Each suit includes a custom-made label with the customer's name woven in—an extra that caters to the unique, one-of-a-kind purchase.
- Apply your highest skill to measure each client. Precise instructions to the hand tailors in Hong Kong result in goods that require few alterations at delivery.
- Take care of "can't wait" customers by stocking racks of finished suits, coats, and slacks.
- Bring in your wife to help during busy lunch-time hours. Let customers browse and locate their size in stock suits while you concentrate on fitting and marking suits for alterations.

You pocket the commission, as well as operating profits, in such an operation. Customers like dealing directly with you, the tailor, because they know you will give them a perfect fit. By working at your highest skill, you channel more of the sales price to profits.

Appliance Service and Sales

Harry H—learned the appliance service trade at night in a vocational school and picked up experience as a service mechanic making house calls. But, as a service mechanic, he was neatly trapped in a dead-end job—no place to move up to. With the crush on service complaints, Harry figured customers would pay extra for appliances that included guaranteed personal service. But, rather than compete directly with department stores and discount houses, Harry opened a small *Fix-It Shop.* He started moonlighting—making house calls to repair major appliances in the evenings and on weekends. At other times, he repaired small appliances brought to his shop. Instead of selling only one or two manufacturers' lines, he learned from experience which appliances from each line were best—and sold those. His approach—sell a complete service—the right appliance, installation, and follow-up service as needed. He worked this way—

● Harry established himself as a "known quantity" in the community. He provided straight service with no double-talk. When Harry said an old machine wasn't worth fixing, few argued. To new-appliance customers, Harry laid it on the line—"This machine works best from my experience."

● Installation and operating instructions initiated his superior service program. Unless installation was correct, a machine would soon go on the blink. Or, if the housewife didn't understand an operation, she could louse up the appliance in short order. So, prevention headed off most service problems.

● "No customer pays for service from Harry," was his clincher. Picking the right machine, installing it correctly, and teaching housewives how to operate the machine properly reduced service calls to an almost unbelievable minimum. So, Harry could guarantee no-cost service for up to five years—depending on the machine—and spend very few bucks on service calls. Buying a complete package with guaranteed service obviously appealed to customers—even more than cut prices—as evidenced by Harry's booming business.

HOW YOU CAN PROFIT FROM APPLIANCE SERVICE

● Build your reputation for honest and knowledgeable service. Invest minutes for the future, like this—Suppose a puzzled woman brings in a toaster that won't work. You strip off the shiny cover and find a wire loose from a terminal. Tightening the screw, replacing the cover, and handing back the toaster in working order for "no charge" costs you maybe five minutes—but you bank customer confidence. You can be sure of two things—the customer will return for service and new appliances and she will spread the word—"he didn't charge a cent." Point out major problems, so customers will understand the reasons for charges. Investing in customer confidences can pay bigger dividends than big-space advertising.

● Combine service skill with sales to gain profit from big-ticket appliances. Guaranteed service rather than a big stock of appliances makes the difference. You're not competing with big discounters. Price appliances to include a small markup to cover future service calls. Make sure appliances are installed properly and housewives know how to use them.

● Insist on customers bringing portable appliances in for service. But, service big appliances at home quickly. Most calls take little time and a minimum of parts, but each call offers an opportunity for instructing the housewife on the proper use of appliances.

Service businesses offer easy access because—

● Capital costs can be kept low at first.

● Skills, specialized and in management, can be acquired working for someone else.

● Moonlighting provides an inviting entry road with minimum risk.

● Demand for services is almost unlimited—and still growing.

With so many plus factors, what are some of the minus factors? Why do many service-oriented businesses fail? A study of business failures among service-oriented firms points out the following pitfalls—

● Dissatisfied customers—Unless you can satisfy customers, your service business won't prosper. Building service profits depends on repeat business.

● Insufficient capital—If your service business requires capital, like Benny's stock of ready-made clothes, make sure you can get the money needed to start the business and keep it going until volume builds. Starting on a moonlight basis reduces capital needs for most service businesses.

● Poor management—Many skilled practitioners, from hair stylists to airplane mechanics, know their specialty but don't understand business. Unless you learn fast about controlling costs, particularly overhead, developing shortcuts for productively using your time, and understand marketing, government regulations, and the myriad of factors facing you as the owner-operator, your business turns sour. Operating experience with a successful business is the one best route to management know-how.

● Too little work—Being in business for yourself requires more hours than working for a boss, particularly during start-up periods. Unless you are self-disciplined and motivated, don't attempt to be your own boss.

When you total the pluses and minuses, you'll find that service businesses offer outstanding opportunities for doubling or tripling your income. Opportunities scale upward from these readily attainable levels for the really successful businessman.

PROVEN PROFIT MAKERS FOR SERVICE BUSINESSES

● Find the right opportunity—Look for a service that is too costly for an individual or family. Either the equipment costs too much or the service requires specialized know-how.

● Improve productivity—Services are largely labor-intensive. But, you multiply earnings by using machinery, unique tools, or specialized know-how effectively.

● Build volume with minimum costs—A restaurant may advertise or offer coupons or other inducements to bring customers in the first time. But, unless food and service are good enough to bring customers back again, you won't develop that repeat business you're looking for. All kinds of publicity and volume-building approaches are open to the innovative restaurant manager—happy hours with low-cost drinks, personal calls on groups who meet regularly for lunch, special prices for groups, offering a hall along with a meal to attract meetings, and special parties timed for holidays.

● Combine sales profits with services—Established services naturally lead to sales—as in Harry's appliance *Fix-It-Shop* operation, or Benny's *Hong Kong Tailors.*

● Offer a new-technology service that also cuts costs—"Instant Printing," for example, provides quality copies at low prices. So, a new service business blooms.

● Keep good records—Without accurate costs records, you can't exercise good management.

● Finally—Providing the kind of services with the efficiency and low cost you'd like to buy yourself leads to a successful service business. Put yourself in a customer's position—would you buy your service at your prices?

4

Your Shortcut to a Fortune--
Capital Appreciation

You pay only about half as much income tax on your earnings when you take the capital-appreciation route to your fortune. Here's how: by improving real estate yourself and taking out your earnings as profits taxed as a capital gain, you double your spendable cash earnings—and you do it in big pieces for a fast return. Capital appreciation lets you exercise your imaginative and management-oriented skills plus buying and selling talent, in a unique combination of elbow grease and smart planning. Capital-appreciation businesses you can work at part time or full time include—

- *Rehabilitating houses for resale where you benefit from financial leverage to increase your profits.*
- *Taking over and refurbishing houses for rent to build your own real estate empire one house at a time— where cash flow sheltered from taxes accelerates your empire building.*
- *Upgrading apartments to increase their resale and/or income-producing value—terrific opportunities for part-time application of do-it-yourself skills.*
- *Rescuing and rebuilding a dying business for capital gains.*
- *Cashing in on the zooming demands for mobile-home parks.*
- *Building a service business and selling out or merging for a big, all-at-once profit.*

Put a package worth of pennies together and sell it for dollars! That's the capital appreciation route you can follow to big money *fast*. Mostly, such ventures involve mind-bending risks, marketing know-how, tubs of elbow grease, and a creative spark of entrepreneurship. When you shoot for capital appreciation, you build synergism where the whole is worth more than the sum of the parts.

Check these quick-cash marks of capital appreciation operations. You get more spendable cash because you pay less income tax on the net gain.

- Value grows faster than cash outlay.
- Sweat equity builds in value with a minimum of cash—a major factor in revaluing real property.
- Psychological revaluation of a property pays enormous dividends.

You have probably seen a Cinderella transformation happen right in your own neighborhood. An old, run-down house goes begging for a buyer even at a cut price. But, fresh paint, lawn and grounds that complement the house, and a clean—CLEAN—interior buoys a buyer. The difference in value greatly exceeds the cost of changing the look. That difference can become your profit.

Creative, imaginative, and cost-saving ideas, sweat-equity, and know-how control the size of your profit payoff more than cash investment. You need imagination and vision to see opportunity for profit in a dismal house or a failing business. Take your cue from the following examples.

REHABILITATING HOUSES

Two well-proven paths can lead you to big-money profits in housing. These two routes are particularly adapted for the moonlighting handyman. First, we'll see how two profit builders operate. They will show you step-by-step how you can do the same.

Rebuilding a House for Resale

Ted S retired from his job as a supervisor of personnel for a major company at age 46 with the profits he earned rebuilding homes for resale. Leverage and "SEM"–somebody else's money–combined to multiply Ted's profits while he invested a minimum of his own funds. Leverage works like this:

Ted S buys a house with a potential market value of $20,000. But, the house's run-down condition attracts no buyers, even at a cut price of $18,000. An existing mortgage on the property has been paid down to $16,000. Ted offers $16,000, is refused, and finally after some shrewd bargaining, buys the house for $16,500. Ted's investment–$500 with $16,000 of SEM in the assumed mortgage. Renovating the house takes six months of Ted's spare time plus $400 for materials, paint, grass seed, lumber, and miscellaneous hardware. Ted and his family live in the house during the six months. After six months, Ted sells the upgraded house for $20,000. Ted clears $3,000 net profit on a total investment of $1,000 plus sweat equity for six months. That is a 600 per cent return on his own money (annual basis). Plus he lived rent-free in the house for six months, paying only on the mortgage interest. Further, the $3,000 profit was a capital gain, so he paid regular income tax on only $1,500. In his 30 per cent bracket, that amounted to $450 tax. Ted worked at his part-time business like this: He searched out houses in neighborhoods on their way up that could be bought for bargain prices. Perhaps the owner transferred. A dull market left the house vulnerable to a ridiculously low offer. Or, a house suffered from disrepair– weedy lawn, shrubs half-dead, peeling paint, possibly a leaky roof, floors and interior in need of rehabilitation. Ted usually bought sizeable houses in the middle-income bracket.

When he bought a house, Ted moved his family in and started to work. In addition to earning living expenses, keeping overhead low, and meeting the "principal residence" require- ment, living in a house allowed Ted to work on the house at odd moments. He planned improvements and shopped for low-cost materials himself. He occasionally hired high school student muscle power for such work as replanting shrubs or rebuilding a lawn. Ted's family helped out occasionally by painting interior walls. He looked particularly for houses with expansion space in either the basement or attic. Such a ploy enabled Ted to buy a three-bedroom house and sell a five-bedroom house. Ted would build living areas into those spaces to attract large families looking for more space. Specific value-adding ideas Ted practiced were—

● Refinishing floors—With a rented floor sander, Ted would completely redo hardwood floors before he moved the family in—so there was less furniture to move about or protect from the dust. If the floors were carpeted in some rooms, he cleaned them with a rented do-it-yourself shampoo outfit at first. Later, he sometimes recarpeted badly worn or damaged areas, laying the carpet himself. Resilient tile floors in bad shape were simply ripped up and replaced.

● Lawns and shrubs affect a potential buyer's first impression. So, plantings and grounds received major attention in season. Sometimes plowing up an old lawn and rebuilding it from scratch took less time and cash than patching. He rented a tractor for the heavy work and hired strong-back students for hand raking, fertilizing, and seeding. Ted dug up native plants from approved wild areas or bought surplus stocks directly from the nursery at less than wholesale prices.

● Exterior painting A new color scheme, or at least a fresh coat of paint all over paid big dividends. One coat usually covered. Gutters and downspouts were patched and painted. A complete reroofing seldom paid dividends but roof leaks, if any, were patched.

● Interior rehabilitation—In addition to floors, rooms were painted or papered to hide water marks from leaks or to cover repairs. Paint, according to Ted, increased value faster relative to cost than any other single item, adding greatly to eye appeal and boosting the psychological value of a house. Ted could paint a room in a day at a cost of less than $6 per room.

● Miscellaneous repairs—Doors that didn't close, cabinets with broken latches, a furnace with a stack plugged with soot or filters filled with lint, and locks that didn't work were all fixed. Broken concrete or cracked basement walls were patched. Plumbing that broadcasted odd noises, faucets that leaked, joints in showers or around tubs that obviously leaked, and toilets that "ran" were repaired to operate reliably.

● Storage added—Any trash or rubbish was cleaned out of potential storage areas in garage, basement, attic, and odd corners of the house. Storage attracts potential buyers—particularly women—all out of proportion to costs. Ted added inviting storage units by—

—Covering wall studs in a garage with perforated hardboard to simplify hanging storage.

—Flooring across the joists in a garage for out-of-season storage.

—Building shelves into closets or basement areas.

—Developing cabinet space in unused floor space.

Through bitter experience, Ted found that certain items were not cost-effective. A few of these low-return items include—

● Extensive remodeling—Rearranging walls, completely remodeling a kitchen, adding rooms that required new foundations or a change in the roof line, and building on complete units, such as a garage or screen porch, cost too much for the value they added.

● Major changes in plumbing or wiring—Such changes seldom showed, so Ted avoided them. If his thorough inspection showed a house obviously needed replacement or extensive additions to plumbing or wiring, he didn't buy the house.

● Structural faults—Rotted sills or joists, seriously cracked foundations, and badly leaking basements require major expenses for correction, so Ted avoided such problems. Ted insisted that the seller furnish a certification that the house was termite-free.

Ted figured he could generate more cash by tackling different kinds of houses. But, he concentrated on moderately expensive houses which could be rehabilitated at minor expense because—

● He lived in the houses during rehabilitation. He wasn't prepared to exist in substandard, cramped quarters while working on the house.

● Minor expenses for paint, shrubs, grass seed, shelf lumber, and miscellaneous hardware and parts, plus his own do-it-yourself know-how, provided a cost-effective return for labor and dollars. Ted counted mainly on the new psychological value improvement resulting from a house's "new look."

● Major remodeling required more man-hours than he could spend moonlighting. Ted preferred to turn the houses over quickly to earn more on the money he had invested.

Fixing Up Houses for Rent

George McD—plays a different variety of the housing rehabilitation game. He is building an investment program for early retirement through rental housing. Rather than operate in the moderate-cost home field, as Ted S— did, George prefers low-cost houses in expanding nonblighted areas. George frequently takes over a house at no cost to himself by agreeing to pay off the outstanding mortgage. Owners frequently owe more on their homes than they could sell them for, particularly if the home has been allowed to deteriorate from neglect. George picks up the house, cleans it thoroughly from ridge pole to basement floor, freshens the paint, puts plumbing and electrical service back in shape, rehabilitates the exterior, and offers it for rent. The economics of the operation work out like this:

Cash flow from depreciation puts tax-free money in George's pocket. Depreciation amounts to a return of capital. In the real estate game this money is "sheltered." George uses the cash flowing from one house to invest in another house. By adding at least two houses a year, he is building income and retirement benefits. Note major differences in approach between Ted S—and George McD—

● George does not live in a house during its rehabilitation. Therefore, he rushes a house into minimum rental condition. Cleaning and repainting take the most time. He also corrects any items that won't work, such as appliances, furnace, or plumbing.

● Maintenance is required regularly because George continues to own the houses. When a tenant reports a roof leak or a broken window, George fixes the problem himself. Only occasionally will he hire a plumber or electrician for a major job, usually when he is fully occupied at another house. George schedules major maintenance, such as replacement of a tile floor or installation of a new range, during temporary vacant periods. Often the promise to correct such a fault clinches a tenant's decision to move in.

● Although he seldom requires a lease, George collects the first and last months' rent—before allowing a tenant to move in.

● George finds tenants without the help of Realtors and with a minimum of advertising by notifying the personnel department of several plants when a house is available, putting a sign on the lawn, tacking notices to free bulletin boards, and using plant newspapers that print free notices of houses for rent.

● Complete and detailed bookkeeping help George control costs of his operations and substantiate tax returns. George maintains his own books, as he is an accountant by trade, but he recommends bringing in a moonlighting accountant to help if you are not an accountant.

Low-Cost Houses Rebuilt

Refurbishing houses for resale need not be limited exclusively to men. Mrs. Laurie C—operates her own college financing program by helping her boys work their way through college. She refurbishes houses for resale much like Ted S—, except that she and her sons do not live in the houses. When her husband died, Laurie C—reckoned that strong measures would be necessary if her three sons expected to graduate from college. So, while her oldest boy was still in high school, she bought her first beat-up house and restored it to a saleable condition.

Mrs. C—personally inspects the houses before buying. Her "thing" is restoration of appearance. Therefore, she looks out for framing that may be rotten, major cracks in the walls that may indicate foundation settling, and inoperable heating or plumbing systems. Any major problem rules a house out. She may examine eight to ten houses before buying one. When buying through a Realtor, Mrs. C—prefers to take over the existing mortgage to keep her interest and closing costs to a minimum.

As soon as the purchase agreement for a house is signed and before closing, Mrs. C—and her boys devise their plan for refurbishing the house. Their aim—restore the house and sell it as quickly as practical. Since the house is not being lived in, interest on the mortgaged value becomes a cost to be charged against any profit.

Mrs. C—and the three boys pitch in to restore the house when she signs the papers. She scrounges during the day for paint, lumber, and other materials plus shrubs if needed. Evenings and weekends, she and the boys work feverishly on the house—painting, patching, and planting. Mainly, they remove accumulated dirt and grime left by former owners. Outside, the lawn is fertilized to restore its lush green growth. In season, annual flowers are planted and shrubs are set out to enhance first-look appeal.

Only when the house is ready for showing, does Mrs. C—begin her marketing plan. From experience she knows how to use every free listing or bulletin board in the area. She sets out her own "Open House" signs to attract lookers on Sunday afternoon. Although she sells the houses herself, she may "cooperate" with Realtors by offering them her bottom price. Anything they can sell the house for above that price is theirs.

When a house is sold, Mrs. C—and her boys divide the net take. Profits amount to the difference between the original cost plus expenses and the net sale price. Each boy shares the profit pie according to the number of hours he put in. Mrs. C—keeps a part of the profit as working capital. Ordinarily, the C—family turns over at least four houses per year with a net profit of from $2,000 to $5,000 on each house. On a per-hour basis, these profits amount to as much as $12 to $16 per hour spent. Mrs. C—reduces the impact of taxation at regular income rates by splitting off the gains to each of the boys. So, they pay tax at near minimum personal rates.

Upgrading Apartments

On a bigger scale, Don S—takes on apartment houses for renovation. Later, he sells the whole unit on an income-producing basis. Older apartments qualify as ripe for restoration when many new apartments are being built in an area. Short-term dwellers with disposable income then move from old apartments with tiny, dark kitchens, into the newer complexes that may include swimming pools, saunas, hobby shops, and the like. Older apartment houses attract tenants only by lowering rentals—so, attract older people on fixed incomes, hippies, part-time workers, etc. Vacant units and low rentals combine to drop gross income. As the property value drops as an income producer, the apartment becomes a prime candidate for upgrading.

Don S—tackles an apartment house as a long-term project. He and his wife move into the manager's apartment and personally run the complex. Living on-site not only saves on living expenses but places him squarely in charge of managing the system—with firm control of every function from renting and collecting rents to removing trash. He tackles one apartment at a time. He makes no structural changes that require moving walls if possible. But, on one project, he took out a wall between a small kitchen and a small dining room and replaced it with a counter-high partition. The open space made both rooms seem larger.

Floors and walls get a full treatment. Rather than play around with the hardwood floors, he installs wall-to-wall carpeting in living, dining, and bedrooms. In one apartment house, he installed a bathroom carpet to cover floors of badly cracked ceramic tile. New resilient tiles in light colors add spirit to the kitchen. Windows get a varied treatment, all aimed at getting more light into the rooms.

Kitchens get priority attention. Old kitchens no longer meet modern standards and fail to satisfy working housewives who buy convenience food and shop once a week. In one apartment house, he ripped out an old-style central refrigeration system and brought in new, self-contained refrigerators with more space and freezer compartments. Counters and cabinets may be completely replaced along with a new range-oven-storage combination. Don aims to consolidate appliances, dress up counter surfaces, and build in more storage.

One frame-built, three-story apartment complex looked so bad from the outside, Don decided on a complete renovation. Small windows were ripped out and replaced with big, easily opened, metal-frame picture windows. To cover the new construction, he covered the old, cracked, dingy wood siding with modern, low-maintenance stained cedar. The apartments looked brand new when he finished—at a fraction of the cost of all-new construction. To go along with the new look, he added a swimming pool in the center court. As a result, the occupancy rate jumped from 55 per cent to 94 per cent; at the same time, he increased room rentals a whopping 30 per cent.

The formula for buying or selling apartment houses runs like this: Multiply the monthly gross receipts times 100. Or multiply annual gross receipts times 8 or 8½. Gross income usually breaks down as follows: taxes and mortgage payment 32-35 per cent; maintenance 10 per cent; vacancy allowance 10 per cent; and expenses (heat, management, advertising, and others) plus profit 45 per cent.

Renovating houses or apartments involves risks that few big builders care to assume. Why? Because profits depend on the know-how and personal involvement of an innovative, decisive entrepreneur right at the scene. Rehabilitation must be fast and leave little room for mistakes. Large builders with many unmotivated workers, unproductive overhead, and ponderous decision-making procedures seldom profit from such unplannable, shoot-from-the-hip operations. But, if you are an active, knowledgeable handyman manager, working largely by yourself, you too can bundle up quantities of cash by using such cost-cutting tactics as—

> ● Performing your own repairs and maintenance—Learn about painting, plumbing fixtures, floor refinishing, and simple electrical repairs. Look for practical help in one of the mechanical magazines, such as *Popular Mechanics* or their *Do-It-Yourself Encyclopedia.*
> ● Bartering for services and equipment—The accountant who renovates houses for rent occasionally needs major plumbing service. So, he keeps a small plumber's books in exchange for plumbing service.

● Collecting all rents—Pattern collections to coincide with renters' paydays, and be there when they have the money to pay.

YOUR STEP-BY-STEP GUIDE TO A FORTUNE IN REFURBISHING REAL ESTATE

Experience and know-how make the difference between turning a heady profit in the fix-up-and-sell (or rent) business— or bombing out. But, you can learn by moonlighting as both Ted S—and George McD did. Follow these basic steps and learn as you earn—

Buy the Right House

Buying right means buying potential—

● Location critical—Neighborhoods move up or down dynamically. Select houses in growing or near-stable areas—never one headed for blight. Check proximity to school, tax burden, transportation, etc. When you buy, look ahead to the time you'll be selling.

● Evaluate a house relative to its neighbors—A small house in a neighborhood of more expensive homes draws value from its surroundings. A run-down, poorly maintained house in a neighborhood where owners take pride in their home picks up value fast when brought up to neighborhood standards.

● Time purchases—Buy houses when prices are seasonally low during the first three months of the year. Sell near peak values in July and August. Buy more than one house at a time only if you can rent them. But, a backlog of houses rented to pay for mortgage, insurance, and taxes earns depreciation and permits greater flexibility than buying one house only when another is sold.

●Use real estate agents to buy, but not to sell—Realtors can put you next to more good houses than you could look at yourself. But, save the 6 or 7 per cent commission by selling yourself.

●Check FHA office—Homeowners who move into an FHA-guaranteed home with a small down payment sometimes walk out with a number of payments due. So, the FHA ends up with a house on its hands. Often these houses need many repairs. Rather than hire a contractor to fix up the house for resale, the FHA may elect to sell a house "as is." These FHA "discount houses" can be good buys for renovation.

Keep Capital Costs Low

Use SEM wherever possible and keep expenses to a minimum with these proven tactics—

● Take over existing mortgages wherever possible—Long-standing mortgages tend to call for low interest rates, so monthly payments are less than refinancing. Also, closing costs less with no new mortgage involved.

● Buy "no down" houses—Lend your credit rating by taking over mortgage with no down payment. With low down payments, market value many times will be less than mortgage—so owner gets out from under his obligation without a penalty when you assume mortgage.

● Work with a mortgage lender to keep lines of credit open—Mortgage companies lend money for financing at low rates or may permit you to take over an existing mortgage when a house may produce a loss. The company then refinances the mortgage for the eventual buyer after you put the house back in saleable condition.

Buy Low-Cost Materials

Here's where your scrounging, innovative ideas pay off, because you need materials to supplement sweat equity in rebuilding value. Try these ideas for starters—

● Buy paint, floor coverings, caulks, wallpaper, and trim at a surplus stock outlet. Brand-name paints may sell for $1.79 a gallon rather than $8.50 or more at a store offering custom mixing. Vinyl floor roll goods may sell for $2.69 a square yard, instead of $9.50. Quality may be first line, but these stores also sell off-brands and seconds, particularly in carpets—so, stay alert to actual value. Mostly stocks are manufacturers' overruns or from bankrupt stores.

● Buy used wrecked components—Houses wrecked for freeways or business building yield sinks, bathtubs, kitchen ranges, pipe, faucets, locks, cabinets—practically everything a remodeler needs at a fourth to a third of new price. Look under "Surplus" in your telephone directory for used building component dealers. Also check for "damaged in transit" materials, appliances, cabinets, and flooring.

● Pay cash for new materials—Small builders and painters fall among the country's worst credit risks. So, selling for cash permits some dealers to cut prices sharply on cash-and-carry sales. These same suppliers frequently carry "seconds" or "irregulars" of doors, plywood, or paneling—at 25 to 30 per cent savings.

● Maintain precise records—Unless you really understand accounting, hire a moonlighter to keep books while you concentrate on controlling cash. You must keep bills, receipts, and labor records for audit. Depreciation for cash flow must follow complex regulations. You may fumble while learning repairs, but you can't afford to fumble your records.

HOW TO BUILD AND SELL A BUSINESS FOR BIG EARNINGS

Real estate and houses or apartment buildings are not the only avenue for capital appreciation ventures. Whole businesses are bought and sold like stocks to acquire capital gains and more spendable cash.

Kinder's Drive-In

This was a one-way stop along Mike Kinder's road of bought-and-sold businesses. He first noted the drive-in's profit possibilities when he stopped in for a quick lunch. The food and service were on a par—both bad! Location and buildings were tops—but the food and service—ugh! Experienced in managing restaurants, he suspected trouble. A few inquiries proved his suspicions—the drive-in was losing money—and fast. With a loss instead of an earnings record, Kinder bought the business by assuming the owner's debts.

Immediately upon taking over, Kinder put his own name on the drive-in and erected "Under New Management" signs and posters. He advertised a *Grand Opening Special* to let people know things had changed. He also fired the so-called cook and replaced him with the chef from a restaurant formerly owned by Kinder. The key—a bonus arrangement enabling the chef to participate in any profits generated.

A "chef" in a drive-in? Of course! Part of the new image! Kinder reasoned that competing head-on with several franchised fast-food outlets was fruitless. So, he and the new chef revitalized the menu to offer full dinners and a take-out window for anything on the menu. The chef brought more than his culinary art to his business. He also knew where and how to buy, how to dicker with suppliers, how to make the most of left-over food, and how to supervise kitchen and waitress help.

Kinder's Drive-In immediately turned back toward a profitable operation. Within one year Kinder had taken all of his cash out of the business, paid back a part of the loan to the bank, and was looking for another opportunity.

Why, where, and how do such business opportunities develop? How can you find and take advantage of them? Check these important considerations—

   ● Selling (and buying) price depend mainly on profits—Either of two methods establish the selling price for a business—capitalized earnings or asset value. Suppose the drive-in had been earning a profit of $15,000 yearly after all costs, including a salary for the manager. Capitalizing earnings according to risk might call for a return of investment (ROI) over five years, or a 20 per cent capitalization rate. $15,000 divided by .20 equals a $75,000 price tag. If the drive-in had been built on a lease (no asset value for the land) and the building plus fixtures were valued at $60,000, the difference between asset value and capitalized price ($15,000) is usually noted as "goodwill." In Kinder's case, the image of bad food and service decreased the value of assets (so, created "badwill"). The owner lost $20,000 of this equity by getting into a business he knew little about.

   ● Kinder immediately began to erase the drive-in's poor image. He realized that, unless he did something drastic, the "badwill" created by the former owner would run him into the ground as well.

   ● Good food remains paramount in any restaurant operation, so Kinder brought in a man he knew was good—then motivated him for top performance by cutting him into a piece of the action.

● Noting the hotly competitive environment for fast take-out food, Kinder and the chef decided on a full-meal policy despite the drive-in operation. Actually, by retaining a take-out window, he covered both bets. The full menu attracted an older, more affluent crowd who still wanted fast service.

When the drive-in turned the corner into a profitable operation, Kinder agreed to sell his interest to the chef. Although the chef had little cash, he agreed to pay Kinder $30,000 for his interest over a five-year period and assume the bank loan. Note that Kinder invested none of his own cash in the venture. He agreed only to pay off the bank loan of the former owner. When he sold out, he picked up a profit of $30,000 plus 8 per cent interest, and shifted the loan to the chef. Kinder paid only for food and wages during the first month out of his own pocket. These costs were repaid quickly out of earnings.

Buying or developing businesses for sale earns capital gains rather than operating profits. Such package deals can be highly profitable if you thrive on big risks with potentially big payoffs. Remember, conservative businessmen with money will invest in a profitable, going business even though they can't start one from scratch. These businessmen have cash, and they hire managers with know-how but little money. A proven, going business involves less risk and offers a calculable profit—better, they figure, than they could get from investing their money in the stock market or real estate. Your job—

- ● Find that business.
- ● Turn the business into a profit maker.
- ● Sell out to capitalize earnings.

Mobile-Home Park

Follow this step-by-step example of how Bart F—turned several minuses into a big plus profit for himself:

Lake-Vista Court was built on what had been a sanitary land-fill site. Once filled, the site was no longer useable by the private rubbish collector. But, a lake view made the site a prime and expensive property for housing. Local builders shied away because of possible problems with settling of the land fill.

Bart F—reasoned that a mobile-home court would solve two problems—high land cost and insensitivity to possible settling. Mobile homes could rest on pads, patios could be laid with blocks, and underground sewer and water facilities could be designed to compensate for settling. So, he leased the property (thereby minimizing capital outlay), erected plug-in facilities for trailer homes, landscaped the property to match the lake-view setting, and began renting spaces. Bart correctly calculated the drawing power of the view and public beach within easy walking distance. His tasteful planning, location, and the community building drew patrons at premium prices. When all spaces were taken, he was taking out a monthly profit of $12,000 over and above his salary and all expenses, including interest on money borrowed to erect facilities. Bart's investment was $40,000. With $144,000 annual earnings capitalized at 12½ per cent, he sold out to a property management firm for $1,152,000 for a gain of $712,000 after paying off a $400,000 loan and his own investment. Not bad, and most of the investment was SEM. Demand for mobile home space is booming. But patrons want more than a pad and hookup. They want a pool, a clubhouse, and many of the same amenities enjoyed by apartment dwellers. An unusual package, including a view like Lake Vista, can turn a neat profit if handled right.

A Sure Profit from a Supermarket

Two brothers, Elmer and Clyde S—, built a local chain of supermarkets by pyramiding a small, independent market into five huge, fiercely competitive markets through hard work and their management know-how in the business. Most of their capital was SEM—but they had proven they knew their business by operating their first small market at a profit. The brothers adopted their plan to build the supermarket chain specifically for sale by—

● Recognizing that they would work hard themselves for at least five years to achieve the big payoff. They did everything around the first small market   stocking shelves at night; buying and displaying top-quality fresh vegetables from early-morning trips to the produce market; buying, ageing, and selling extra-quality meat at competitive, volume prices.

● Borrowing up to the limit of their credit to open a brand-new supermarket near their first store. Shrewd advertising, no-profit specials, and a hot-bake shop combined with a snack bar brought in customers by the thousands.

● Opening a second, and three more stores in turn, at the rate of one a year—all on SEM borrowed on the basis of their profitable operation. Bankers willingly loan money to businessmen who prove they can use it profitably.

● Selling out to an expanding national chain on the basis of their proven profit record. The brothers' private five-year plan paid off handsomely in cash they could keep through capital gains tax treatment. Neither of them need work again because of the fortune they built with hard work and know-how.

The intricacies of buying or developing a business and selling out for a capital gain involve more detailed analysis and planning than can be detailed in one chapter. An excellent, detailed, and easy-to-understand volume that covers most points is available from the Small Business Administration—*Buying and Selling a Small Business.*

5

Capitalize Your Technical Know-How--Break Away for Independence

---

Technically based new businesses develop outstanding pro-fits for innovators and engineers. Further, going into business may be the only route open for frustrated scien-tists, inventors, and engineers. A business of your own helps you escape the big-business trap where financial or mar-keting hot-shots dominate upper management positions. Technically based new businesses enjoy unique attributes, such as—

- *High survival rates—once started, technical com-panies tend to prosper and grow.*
- *Easy access to capital—new technology companies are the darlings of Wall Street when they grow to the point of "going public" with stock offerings.*
- *Little competition in the beginning because of a unique invention or personal know-how by the founder-operator.*
- *Inventors who sell production rights to their develop-ments to small companies for cash and continuing royalties.*
- *Major industries, such as computing, open multiple supporting service requirements—and requirements lead to new businesses for motivated people with special skills.*

If you are an engineer or scientist, you probably consider yourself a team worker. Massive capital, expensively equipped laboratories, and varied staff support appear necessary for developing and producing technical products. Yet, every year, technical innovators and creative scientists break away from big business and go it alone. You can follow the path of these scientific pioneers or inventors and find your fortune—as they have done.

Areas around Boston are dotted with spin-offs from Massachusetts Institute of Technology. Two researchers started Digital Equipment, for example, with $75,000—much of it borrowed. Ten years later the company was worth $240 million—and it is still growing. Some spin-offs grow so big, they spawn spin-offs of their own as creative scientists seek a bigger share of profits from their own inventiveness. Technically based companies carve unique niches in small business enterprises for a number of reasons.

Survival of newly formed technical companies (about 80 per cent after ten years) remains about four times higher than for other business types. The reasons for high survival? Three reasons stand out—

1. A no-nonsense approach by analytical engineers.
2. A start by most technical spin-offs as moonlighting operations.
3. Requirements for large quantities of capital.

Along with the money, comes financial advice and controls. Although financial controls may frustrate the creative engineer at times, they assure good management of that key commodity, money.

- Money for new, high-technology companies can be raised with remarkable ease. Money from stock offerings or investment companies is often readily available to those new organizations which can demonstrate a high potential for growth. A new stock offering with "electronic" or "computer" in the company name sells quickly to investors eager to get in on the ground floor for projected growth.
- Spin-off companies result from innovators, inventors, or developers who were frustrated in their big-company associations.

Research and development (R&D) organizations in big companies often suffer hardening of the arteries with time. Caution and indecision replace initiative and creativity. Individuals with bold ideas are smothered. An idea must traverse a tortuous route to approval by management. So, the excited, "turned-on" engineer soon loses patience. He develops his idea in his basement shop and organizes his own company to market the product. Some ideas are so specialized or so unrelated to the company's product line that the company prefers not to pursue the product potential. But, such an idea may be just the thing for a small company.

● Better payoff for truly creative engineers can come about. As a team member, a brilliant innovator carries his team. But, by overhead and benefit splits to other, less productive team members, he dilutes his own money rewards. Only a few key inventors and innovators in each big company make the difference between growth and decline. Those who stay carry a big load of job hangers-on and staff personnel. But, by starting his own business, the creative engineer who draws a salary closer to the value of his contributions enjoys unparalleled fringe benefits, and his stock interests increase his capital.

● Engineers and scientists carry a wealth of acquired know-how in their heads. By exercising initiative, the technical innovator converts such know-how into a new business.

● Motivation by individuals to improve their status, wealth, and ego-satisfaction leads to successful businesses based on technical know-how.

HOW AIRCRAFT TECHNOLOGY PAYS OFF

STOL Modifications

Not every engineer, designer, or scientist can come up with an idea as original as Carlson's Xerox copier. But, Robertson Aircraft grew from one man's technical know-how and enterprise. James L. Robertson worked for several aircraft companies before starting his own firm. Robertson Aircraft modifies Cessna and other small airplanes for STOL (Short Takeoff and Landing) operations into and out of short airfields. Modification costs begin at $4,000 per airplane and move up. A mod requires only about three days to install. Yet, the company modifies up to 15 airplanes per month and is pointed at $1.5 million in yearly sales with a 50-per cent annual growth rate projected.

Modifying airplanes can be tricky because a company may run out of customers. But, Robertson used publicity effectively rather than advertising. Now, customers come from all over the world. Kits are being installed by licensed dealers on every continent. The modifications, of course, are unique for each airplane type and were developed from Robertson's creative technical expertise. One Alaskan flier used his STOL-modified Cessna to fly into and out of a 275-foot-long lake—about as big as an oversize swimming pool. The Robertson-inspired modifications reduce stall speed and permit steep-angle approaches and climb-outs. The relatively minor cost for modification converts one of ten standard Cessnas to a STOL airplane, comparable to an airplane costing as much as $90,000.

Why doesn't the factory incorporate the mods on its own production line? First, Robertson patented his developments. Second, the STOL-modified airplanes account for only about 5 to 10 per cent of the market, too small for factories interested in mass producing airplanes. Specialized models accrue excessive overhead for design. Also slipping in a few odd-ball airplanes disrupts the smooth flow of the assembly line. By keeping costs low, Robertson Aircraft can price its modification package under the big makers' price schedules. In addition to ten Cessna models, Robertson is already aiming at Piper, Beech, and Aero Commander airplanes. With 5 to 10 per cent of 80,000 airplanes as candidates for modification, the STOL-mod market is not likely to dry up.

Robertson began by designing STOL modifications for one Cessna airplane while continuing to work for The Boeing Company. The modifications resulted from Jim's experience with advanced high-lift technology. Jim Robertson was only a few credit hours away from a Doctorate in aeronautical engineering. So, he combined theory with practical experience, always a good combination. The modifications he devised for the first Cessna included an extended, curved leading edge to guide airflow over the wing during high-angle-of-attack flight at slow speeds, top surface stall "fences," revised trailing-edge flap system along with drooped ailerons, and a spring-loaded device for trimming the elevator system. Altogether, the STOL mods added only 18 pounds to the Cessna.

Robertson first modified a flying demonstrator. Flights in the demonstrator so startled technical magazine editors, who were also pilots, that they spread the word worldwide. The demonstrator also performed tests for the Federal Aviation Administration to certify the modifications as safe and reliable. A Supplementary Type Certificate (STC) is mandatory before the modified airplanes can be sold. About a third of the airplanes to be modified are flown directly to the Bellevue Airfield from the Cessna production line. The whole operation requires only 28 employees. Some parts are manufactured under contract. Other parts are fabricated in a separate manufacturing division. Robertson installs the parts at an assembly area in New Orleans, Louisiana, as well as the Bellevue factory.

Robertson's big costs involve design and development, along with many expensive flight tests. Another big cost is the certificate flight demonstrations required to earn the all-important STC approval by the Federal Aviation Administration. Each new airplane type being modified must be certified separately by demonstrating full performance in the air. Flight training for owners requires about two hours of side-by-side training. Nevertheless, the two-year-old company cleared more than 16 per cent gross profit the second full year of operation.

Robertson Aircraft's success highlights several factors affecting technical spin-offs—

● Modifying existing airplanes opens small business opportunities where starting a new airplane company would require capital and organization far beyond an individual's capability. An individual, with specialized technical know-how, can find a small niche and enlarge its potential to gain major financial success. Robertson Aircraft's success came from making a big improvement in airplane performance for a modest cost.

● Financial rewards from starting his own firm afforded Robertson far greater benefits than continuing to work for Boeing.

● Effective use of publicity and word-of-mouth advertising built a worldwide business that is continuing to expand. Robertson spent only $3,000 on direct advertising. Publicity came from articles in technical magazines.

● By keeping overhead low, jobbing out manufacture of many parts requiring expensive machinery, and sticking to what he knew best, Robertson maximized his potential. Attempting to set up a complete factory might have swamped the business before it started.

● A superior product at a competitive price protects the market. Robertson Aircraft operates under the price umbrella of the big airplane companies with their high overhead. By staying small and efficient, he can always underprice such big competitors.

STEP BY STEP TO A FORTUNE-BUILDING TECHNICALLY BASED BUSINESS OF YOUR OWN

You can follow the highly successful step-by-step route used by Jim Robertson and other engineers and scientists to develop your own business.

Establish a Market

Improved technology constantly develops needs—or your idea may fulfill a need barely recognized. Ask yourself these questions

● Can your idea or invention do an existing job better for less cost?

● Will it do something not now being done—for which there is a need?

● Who is your competition?

● Why is your competition not building and marketing your idea?

● What will it take to reach the market you wish to serve?

Let's look at Robertson Aircraft's approach. Airfield facilities limit the usefulness of light airplanes in many areas. Alaska, Canada, and many of the Asian, African, and South American countries contain few developed airports. So, airplanes fly into short, cleared strips. Airstrips cost multi-bucks to develop so, if strips can be short, they cost less. Jim Robertson researched the need for years. He KNEW that an inexpensive airplane capable of flying into and out of short, austere airfields would attract buyers from mining and oil-exploration companies—plus many others. He surveyed the competition—STOL airplanes were available, but at very high prices—several times the cost of ordinary light airplanes. Finally, he knew that private flyers circulate—they get around, and they love to talk. So, if he could develop his STOL airplane, he felt he could market it with little difficulty.

Develop Your Product

Ideas in the head are literally "a dime a dozen." Most people, buyers, financiers, lawyers, and others, will not react to arm-waving descriptions. They want to see and evaluate hardware. So, you must develop your idea into a working, demonstrable model.

Jim Robertson designed the hardware he needed literally on the backs of envelopes. A designer friend and associate converted Jim's concept sketches to engineering drawings. While continuing to work days for The Boeing Company, Jim rented a T-hangar at a nearby Bellevue airstrip. He bought a used high-wing Cessna with borrowed money. The STOL development did not drop out of the sky as a complete package. Each development required fiddling, changing, trying, flying, and further modification before Jim was satisfied. As a pilot, he flew the airplane himself to test the changes. He and his friends spent many nights and weekends modifying the test airplane. Finally, they had developed a full-size airplane with the STOL modifications installed, ready for test and demonstration along with an experimental permit from the FAA.

Organize Your Business

Whether you operate as a proprietorship, partnership, or corporation depends on your product, projected size, and many other considerations. See Chapter 12 for information to guide you on business organization. In addition to an organization format, you need financing, management, marketing, and other special skills. You probably also need help at this point. Consultation and counsel are readily available if you know where to ask—again, see Chapter 12. But, technically based businesses tend to be large and to require considerable capital, so organization—a strong base from which to grow—is important.

Robertson Aircraft was organized as a corporation under the laws of the State of Washington. Jim put up $500 to meet the minimum paid-in capital requirements for a charter. At first he handled all of the organization details himself, hiring a lawyer to draw up the articles of incorporation. Money needs were few before he started volume production. But, with the corporation under way, he was ready to launch Robertson Aircraft.

Market Your Product

Publicity, advertising, and personal sales effort are needed to make potential customers aware of your product and to sell them. The technical press includes many trade and business publications that exist to keep their readers informed of new developments—particularly new ideas that will save money or improve their product competitively. But, closing a sale still requires personal man-to-man communication. You can follow these steps to sell your product—

● Enlist the help of a newspaper or trade magazine to publicize your product. Begin by contacting the business editor of your local newspaper. A local story alerts free-lance writers to develop an article about your product or business in depth. Or, a stringer for a magazine like *Business Week* may pick up the lead and ask you for information. Cooperate in any way possible, because publicity can be worth more than advertising. Supply information, photographs, drawings, and addresses of users. You can hire a public relations firm to handle such contacts, pay a moonlighting free-lance writer to develop publishable stories, or assign one of your own staff to this important function. In marketing technical products or services, there is absolutely no substitute for publicity.

● Invite magazine editors or writers to test and write about your products. Robertson Aircraft's most successful gambit was to encourage aviation writers to fly its STOL-modified demonstrator. Their straight-from-the-cockpit reports quickly spread the word among the magazines' millions of readers—worldwide. In addition to straight performance reports, Robertson continues to earn publicity by developing end-use articles that show how the STOL-mods perform a specific job, such as oil pipeline inspection or flights into a high-altitude South American airfield. A creative publicity writer can develop a wide range of articles magazines will print because they are reader oriented; thereby, qualifying as editorial matter.

● Develop your own sales force to follow up inquiries from publicity or advertising and to personally close sales. Robertson Aircraft sells mainly out of its Bellevue and New Orleans mod centers. Foreign licensees handle their own sales. Manufacturers who sell through hardware stores or to industry may need traveling salesmen and sales branches in strategic locations around the country. Your best bet here is to ask for counsel from a marketing consultant or SCORE (see Chapter 12).

● Employ technically qualified manufacturers' representatives to sell your products as independent agents. You pay them only when they produce sales. You can advertise for manufacturers' agents in technical magazines or contact one of the associations of manufacturers' agents. The associations specialize. Look for the name and address of the one for your technical specialty in the *Directory of Associations* available in most libraries.

● Advertise your products specifically in those magazines read and used by firms or individuals interested in your product. Robertson Aircraft would advertise in *Private Pilot* to reach a high percentage of preselected potential buyers.

● Exhibit in trade shows and technical symposia. Trade shows bring together buyers and producers interested in specialized technology. Your competition will be there, so you better be there too. Follow leads in the trade magazines for the shows that can aid your marketing. If you make boats, exhibit in various regional boat shows. If your product is aimed at industry, exhibit in a show associated with the annual technical meeting of a society. The

Society of Automotive Engineers, for example, sponsors a huge show for suppliers of automotive parts and accessories in connection with the society's annual meeting in Detroit. Hundreds of narrowly specialized technical societies follow the same procedure.

● Consolidate all of your marketing efforts—locating buyers, following up inquiries, providing good service and follow-up, and closing sales. Innovative technical specialists seldom understand the full impact of marketing. So, as soon as finances permit, hire yourself an astute marketing manager and pay him for performance.

Develop Your Long-Range Plan

Technically based companies need to plan growth, new products, and upgraded variations of their products more than most types of businesses—because new products don't stay new for long. Technology companies must develop new products or wither. Details on how to go about developing your long-range growth plan are covered in Chapter 10, along with ideas for gathering the money you need to finance long-range growth.

INVENT YOUR OWN INDEPENDENCE

Larry B. W----fits the classic prototype of inventor. He works in his basement by himself, owns more than 100 patents, and pulls in $100,000 in royalties every year. Yet, he produces nothing for sale but developed ideas. His inventions range from tiny electrical controls in record players to audio components for the weightlessness and high-G accelerations of manned spacecraft. His success hinges on—

● Sticking to one basic field—audio switching devices in W----'s case. Single-field concentration permits intensive developments with a minimum of research. He already knows what has been done because he pioneered most of the unique audio devices. New ideas flow from past experience and a look at new switching requirements.
● Mixing with other engineers for stimulation. Working alone quickly leads to suffocation. Mr. W----deliberately seeks opportunities for talking with other engineers. "They fire me up" he says. "Inspiration may be fine for some, but I get few ideas just sitting."

●Marketing his inventions for manufacture and sale by others. Larry produces nothing and sells only the rights to manufacture his developments for a royalty on sales.

Sell Your Invention to a Company

Whether your invention will be bought by a company or not obviously depends on the invention. But, how you approach a company affects your chances. Generally, you'll find a small company more receptive than a big company. Also, an agent-middleman can help. When you are ready to market your invention, remember—

●Avoid big companies because attempts to sell an invention to a big company seldom pay off. Here's why—big companies maintain their own highly structured research and development (R&D) departments. Plans for new products receive go-ahead approval only after multiple reviews by staffs and management. You'll run into the same frustrations trying to sell your invention as those that drive creative engineers and scientists out of big-company R&D. A big factor is NIH for Not Invented Here. A second factor—your invention may already have been thought of by engineers inside the company. So, big companies build a wall to keep outsiders out.

●Try an aggressive small company; they seldom maintain expensive product development or research laboratories. Instead, small companies depend on individual inventors for new product ideas and openly invite inventors to submit their ideas. Small companies also investigate the offerings at annual inventors' shows in major cities. Address a letter like the one shown in Fig. 5-1 to one small company at a time to explore their interest (see page 104).

Selling Your Idea Through an Agent

As an inventor anxious to patent and sell your idea for cash, take these steps in sequence—

1. Order a copy of *Questions and Answers About Patents* from the Government Printing Office, Superintendent of Documents, Washington, D.C. 20402. This free booklet provides basic information you need to know about getting a patent. Also available from the Superintendent of Documents (but not free) are, *General*

CONFIDENTIAL AGREEMENT LETTER
(Typewritten on Individual or Company Letterhead)

Name of Company
Address

Gentlemen:

 I have invented _____
(Describe invention only in broad terms)

_____

which I believe has considerable commercial merit. If your company wishes to evaluate my invention for possible manufacture and sale, I shall be happy to disclose the details if you will agree to accept their disclosure in confidence, agree not to disclose the details to anyone else, or use the invention for your own gain without specific written authorization from me.

 If this is agreeable with you, will you kindly sign and date this letter where indicated below, and return the same to me, keeping a copy for yourself and indicating when and where we can confer.

Very truly yours,

Your name
Title (if any)

(Name of Company to whom idea is submitted:)

By _____
 (Name of Officer and Title)

Dated: _____

Figure 5-1. *Sample inquiry letter adapted from one used by Research Associates at the Regional Development Laboratory in Philadelphia. See Chapter 12 for more information on the RDL.*

Information Concerning Patents and *Patents and Inventions—An Information Aid for Inventors.* Unless your idea is patentable, you will not be able to license it to a company for manufacture and sales. You can develop, manufacture, and sell a service, product, or technology that is not, by itself, patentable if you do it yourself.

2. Locate an honest patent attorney or patent agent. There is a difference. A patent attorney is, first of all, a lawyer who specializes in patent law. A patent agent knows the ropes about applying for and getting a patent and has passed a test qualifying him to practice within the framework of the Patent Office but he is not a lawyer. The agent will probably charge you less than a lawyer. Supposedly you can get a patent without the help of a patent attorney or agent. Practically no inventor does. How can you locate an honest patent attorney or agent? First, avoid those who advertise. Second, look locally. Your patent agent need not be located in Washington, D.C. Third, inquire among your friends, from your banker, or from a local businessman for leads to a responsible lawyer or agent. Search for a patent attorney or agent the same way you would for a personal lawyer or doctor. Fourth, ask the attorney or agent about his fees. Ordinarily, a patent costs from $800 to $1,600. A legitimate attorney or agent will lay out all costs involved squarely at the beginning.

3. Institute a patent search—cost from $75 to $125. A search cost breaks down into two parts—searcher's fee (in Washington, D.C.) and the attorney or agent's fee. On any bill, your agent should indicate the amount charged for each part.

4. Begin marketing your idea while your patent is pending. A patent pending often affords more protection than an issued patent because the allowed claims are still undefined. Five or more years may elapse before a patent is issued. You can lose valuable time waiting. Instead, pursue these ideas—

—Find a middleman to help you market your invention. These agents operate professionally like theatrical or writers' agents—bringing innovator and manufacturer together for a fee. But—where do you find an honest, aggressive agent or middleman? First, you ask your patent attorney or patent agent. He can put you in touch with a reliable marketing agent or group. Avoid a middleman who wants cash right away or a regular retainer. Instead, look for an agent who will search for a buyer or licensee for a fee payable as a percentage when a contract is negotiated.

—Talk to more than one agent-middleman, if possible. A reliable agent may not be interested in your invention for one or more reasons. Ask a potential agent for his credentials, review his sales record, and check with his clients. But, remember, you will probably need the reliable, successful agent more than he needs you.

—Exhibit your invention in the annual "Inventors Fairs" or similar shows sponsored by a Chamber of Commerce or other group. Small manufacturers visit such exhibitions regularly in search of new products to manufacture. Participation may cost you a fee, but it will be a reasonable one if the show is legitimate. Be prepared for the show—build a working model of your invention, show end uses or potential applications, and prepare a hand-out folder describing your invention. Deals are seldom consummated at the show, so follow-ups are important.

—Ask a local office of the Small Business Administration for help (see Chapter 12). Counselors at the SBA and SCORE consultants regularly offer help and advice to inventors.

COMPUTING — YOUR WIDE-OPEN FIELD

Electronic Data Processing (EDP in the trade) continues to expand rapidly. Niches the size of the Grand Canyon exist for innovators, programmers, and idea developers to exploit. EDP remains far from the exclusive province of the big computer manufacturers, like IBM and RCA. Sure, the big companies make the computers, but processing requires all varieties of programming. Capital requirements can be less for computing technology because the big manufacturers prefer to lease their equipment. Take these examples—

● University Computing Co. of Dallas, grew from one secondhand computer to a $30 million business in only five years. At one look, Sam Wyly's share of the stock in University Computing was valued at a minimum of $60 million. How did Sam and his brother Charles do it? "You find a little bitty thing you can do," Sam Wyly is quoted as saying "and you keep on doing it." The two brothers aimed at building a computer service utility with centers connected to data-transmission lines. The utility would offer a full range of services, including training in computer programming. University Computing not only operates computer centers but leases computers and manufactures accessory equipment. Because of University Computing's growth potential, investors value its stock at unusually high price-earning ratios. The company expanded, quickly acquiring other companies including an insurance company, issuing stock to expand.

● Digital Equipment Corp. took a different tack—developing and selling small computers in a field dominated by giants. Over a ten-year-old period, Digital's sales grew to around $60 million with 12 per cent net profit. Although competition is coming in, the small computer market is expanding faster than the giant computer market dominated by IBM, Honeywell, and General Electric.

● EDP Technology, Inc. develops computer software (programs to operate the computers for specific jobs) and uses EDP for systems analysis. These services require knowledgeable analysts and new developments constantly erode software effectiveness. So, the business runs at a breakneck pace constantly to keep up with technology. Contracts for the company fall in the $30 million-plus yearly category. Software development is labor intensive—and the labor comes high.

● Leasing computers appears to be a deceptively simple business. Leasing firms buy computers from IBM or RCA and lease them to companies like General Motors, American Oil Co., and the like. How can computer leasing companies operate? By offering lower rental fees. Because of the rapid development pace, computers obsolete themselves with disturbing regularity. So, the big makers prefer to sell or to lease them on short terms. Either alternative can be expensive to an operating company. Instead, companies lease computers from a leasing company, like Boothe Computer Corp. When a leased computer is obsoleted by a faster, bigger computer, Boothe may lease the old one to a company that can still use the machine—or sell it through the booming used-computer market.

How can hard-working, computer-smart innovators crack the huge computer-technology market? Take the example of Ikon, Inc. Ikon provides a time-sharing accounting service—mainly payroll processing. Customers feed information into Ikon's computer through *Touch-Tone* telephones. As many as

500 customers may be feeding information into the home computer without interference on a real-time-sharing basis. Ikon handles payrolls for firms with as many as 2,500 employees. The payroll transactions are all pre-programmed—tax withholdings, dues, savings, commissions, after-tax deductions, and final payout are all figured at electronic speed. Checks are printed and mailed out to customers. In addition to printed and signed paychecks, the system also turns out summary accounting records, tax information, and W-2 forms for employees.

Ikon got its start when three partners joined forces. Each was a specialist—one in software development, one in computer hardware, and one in finance. Like so many successful businesses, they started on a moonlighting basis. Among the three of them, they raised or borrowed enough capital to start. They spent $100,000 for an industrial-type computer and programmed it to handle the *Touch-Tone* inputs on real time. Checks and records are delivered 24 hours after inputting. Payroll accounting is only one of the on-line functions available. Ikon expects to program other uses just as fast as time is available.

Opportunities in computing open readily to the trained EDP salesman, programmer, or hardware specialist. Computing technology operates in a closed world with languages like COBOL and FORTRAN. But, once a programmer or a systems analyst comes up with an idea, getting a system going and expanding it once it is operating appears remarkably easy. Like most new, rapidly expanding industries, opportunities in EDP are greater than in established industries. Right now electronic data processing is a wide-open field with millions to be made. No one really knows yet how big the industry is likely to grow—and the business is for youngsters. The oldest of the three partners in Ikon, for example, turned 27 years old when they formed their company.

EXPANDING TECHNOLOGY FIELDS— YOUR KEY TO A FORTUNE

Technology offers unlimited potential for starting your own business—if you possess special qualifications. Just a scattered sample of businesses where innovative, aggressive, technically trained businessmen are carving out their own private fortunes includes—

● *Foto Guard International* markets a patented photographic device that snaps pictures of stickups and manhandling in stores without the knowledge of the toughs or hold-up men. Although started to help small merchants protect themselves, the devices are now being marketed mainly to prevent shoplifting—because merchants cannot buy insurance against pilferage. The National Retail Merchants Association estimates that shoplifting accounts for 2.63 per cent of the price charged for goods by merchants each year . After less than one year in operation in only one part of the country, Foto Guard's business was booming along at a $1 million-per-year clip. Expansion countrywide and into Europe on a franchise basis opened opportunities never dreamed of when the two partners first started.

● All-terrain vehicles (ATV) are being manufactured by more than 50 small companies. These are the small vehicles with big balloon tires or an air cushion that skim over water, swamp, sand, and rough land with equal ease. Fun cars, dune buggies, and mini-hot rods pack a marketing wallop that opens a whole new field to the creative designer-builder. Basically, these ATV and fun cars start with a proven engine and chassis, like the Volkswagen. The designer-builder adds a new body built from fiber glass and plastic. Design, speed, and roughing-it ability are keys to sales. Meyers-Manx, Boon Docker Buggies, Bushmaster, Pizazz, and Mini-T are just a few names in the fun-vehicle business.

● Puget Sound Airlines typifies the small feeder airline now starting or expanding into every part of the United States. More than 250 third-level airlines operate with airplanes that squeeze in under the 12,500-pound limit set by the Federal Aviation Administration. Even smaller are the one- or two-man air-taxi operations that fly on contract or by reservation. Profits for air-taxi and feeder airline companies haven't matched the organizers' enthusiasm to date. Expanded airport facilities and the growing demands for flights into recreational areas are expected to clear the air to profitability.

HOW DO YOU STACK UP?

What are the attributes of relatively young, successful science-based companies? The Regional Development Laboratory of Southeastern Pennsylvania commissioned the Research Department of Industrial Research, Inc. to survey new science-based companies in the Greater Philadelphia area. Samples of their findings include—

● Company founders averaged 35 years of age, held B.S. degrees in science or engineering, and conceived the idea on which their company was founded while employed. The typical founder offered his idea to his employer but found little interest because the product was "not practical" or did not fit into the product line. Initial capital from his savings plus borrowing from friends and relatives averaged $85,000 to start a company, although the figure ranged from under $1,000 to more than $1 million. The desire to be in business for himself motivated the average entrepreneur. His present company was the first he had ever started, and he favored the corporate form of organization.

● New firms surveyed sold an average of $135,000 the first year—and almost turned a profit. When additional capital was needed, a founder borrowed from banks or sold stock to friends. The average company expanded from an original four persons, including the founder and president, to 63 people, including 14 technical professionals. The average company developed ten new products and sales volume grew to $1 million. Operations turned profitable for most of the companies in the second year.

● Founders worked a "relaxed" 55 hours a week following initial organization and start-up. When the company was first formed, the founders averaged 60 hours per week.

● Urgent needs cited among the surveyed companies were surprisingly common. Money and qualified personnel headed the list.

● Marketing was originally handled by the founder, but, since formation of their companies, the founders changed methods to increase use of sales representatives and company salesmen.

● When asked "What factor or quality contributed most to your success?" the following answers were mentioned most often—

1. Hard work and brute-force determination to build a company into a successful venture had to be primary requirements. Luck, technical competence, business sense, and capable supporting personnel were also mentioned as ingredients in the "formula for success."

2. Slightly less than half of the founders held patents and one-fourth considered patents essential to their organizations. A majority of the founders indicated that their products or services were not patentable or patents were not important.

6

Your Fortune May Be in Your Creative Talent

Talented individuals with a yearning for earnings face a difficult choice—creating new and interesting products or producing their creative ideas and skills profitably. To solve this dilemma, learn how to—

- *Turn a flair for designing and producing craft products into a part- or full-time business of your own.*
- *Sell handcrafting for higher prices and quicker production.*
- *Build your own crafts business with supplemental activities—lessons, sales of materials, teaching through writing, and developing new equipment.*
- *Build a talent-based business, like motion picture productions, from your noncraft talents.*
- *Cash in on your hobby.*
- *Help your fellow sportsmen with your talent for outdoor activities.*
- *Promote your craft, hobby, or talent business through publicity and personal appearances.*

Talent—that God-given ability bestowed selectively on individuals—enables you as an artist, designer, jeweler, potter, woodcarver, cameraman, you name it, to develop your own exclusive business. No one else has your specific creative ability. You are unique. But, your talent, be it creative, artistic, analytical, or dramatic, won't suffice by itself. You must backstop your talent with marketing skills, productivity, managerial know-how, and a flair for promotion. Certain skilled hobbies such as woodworking, also qualify as talent business prospects. So, wherever your talents lie, consider these pluses and minuses when you turn your talent or hobby into a paying business—

● Businesses based mainly on talent usually require little capital to start. Talent-based businesses depend on their own unique capital—the talent of the entrepreneur.

● Artists, potters, designers, and others generally start their business on a part-time basis. Hobbies and crafts also form an ideal base for a moonlighting business.

● Earnings ordinarily tend toward the slim side because competition among moonlighters drives prices down. People with talent like to use it—even when they make very little money for their time. So, competition from amateurs holds down professional prices—and profits. But, amateurs play at business. As a professional, you can manage profits through promotion and productivity.

● Productivity provides the key to profits in talent businesses more than in most other kinds of business. Artists, for example, may prefer to "create" rather than "produce." Consequently, they may earn less than their potential when figured on an hourly basis.

TURNING CRAFT ARTISTRY INTO PROFITS

Garrison Originals are items of handcrafted jewelry sold in specialty outlets and gift shops from Florida to Colorado to Seattle's Pike Place Market. Each piece of metal or gemstone jewelry is handcrafted and unique in design. The *Originals* are the work of Leigh and Bill Garrison who create and fabricate rings, earrings, chains, pins, cufflinks, tie-tacks, and other individually distinctive jewelry at their *Studio 714* in Seattle. Two key factors account for their success – productivity and a calculated, handcrafted look about their creations. Bill Garrison tells how these two factors are related.

"Several years ago I took an order for a pair of custom-designed, 18-karat gold earrings, each with a single opal. The stones were souvenirs from a trip to Australia. It was my first really big order, and I wanted to do a superb job. Even though I priced the earrings at $75, I spent so many hours crafting that my time priced out at less than $5 per hour. But the earrings were truly perfect—not a flaw. I was as proud of my work as any mother of her offspring. However, when the lady came to pick up her earrings, she refused to accept them. 'They are too perfect', she said. 'They don't look handcrafted. If I had wanted a perfect job, I could have taken them to any number of places. I wanted *handcrafted* earrings.' Naturally, I reworked them in half the time. When I finished, the pair of earrings were not identical. Prongs holding the opals in their mount were slightly askew and fused with a random look. When the lady came again, she was completely delighted. The earrings looked hand-crafted—and were uniquely styled. It's a lesson I have never forgotten – handcrafted jewelry should look *handcrafted*. *Garrison Originals* are unique and look it. It is not a matter of deliberately making mistakes, but rather of not always making perfect corrections of mistakes."

The Garrisons practice what they call their three "P's"—Productivity Provides Profits. For the skilled craftsman, the desired *handcrafted* look requires less time than trying for a perfect job. So, instead of turning out one ring in three hours, Bill may turn out three rings—similar but with enough subtle differences to retain their original handcrafted look. When pricing reflects time, three rings will obviously bring in more cash than one ring. Bill related a typical flaw in craftwork pricing—

"Suppose a silversmith spends ten hours designing and crafting a superb necklace. In addition to $20 in sterling silver material, the craftsman may value his time at $10 per hour. Therefore, he must sell the piece for $120, and the retailer will mark the piece up to $240. Despite an exploding demand for handcrafted jewelry, pieces priced at $240 sell slower than pieces priced at $120. But, if the craftsman priced the piece at $60 for a markup to $120, he would net only $4 per hour for his time."

Bill's answer is to make three of the pieces in the same time—and that's easily possible with his shortcuts—and by performing each operation on all three items in sequence. Then, he can sell the pieces for $60 each. After allowing the same $20 for materials, the craftsman nets $40 for each piece or $120 total for his ten hours. Instead of $10, he earns $12 per hour.

A craftsman who sells his work himself can net closer to the retail price—but not all of it. *Studio 714* advertises, and customers come in to select from the ready-made jewelry or to order custom mountings for their own gemstones. Such business can be profitable but the cost of maintaining *Studio 714*, of advertising, and the time spent in selling must all be considered in computing profits. The Garrisons do both—sell retail at *Studio 714* and produce their *Originals* for wholesaling to specialty and gift shops.

Garrison's highly successful approach to a creative, artistic business involves the following no-nonsense attributes—

> ● Hard work. Creating individually designed jewelry for sale requires many hours at the bench in order to turn out stock for sales.
> ● Producing items with a minimum of time for each piece to keep prices down and hourly values high. Although each piece may be distinctly handcrafted, Bill may make a dozen or a hundred pieces in one batch. For example—a favorite *Original* is one of several designs of bent-wire, mod-styled, large earrings. The copper, brass, or silver wire may cost little, but the time to craft two earrings by hand for each sale could price them out of the market. So, Bill designs wire-bending fixtures that enable him to form the wire quickly and uniformly but not identically. Each piece retains its own slight but subtle "mistake." He works fast, and a pair of wire-

wounds may take a total of only five minutes per pair when produced in quantity. Extra time at the beginning for design and construction of the wire-bending fixture pays off over many copies.

● Advertising and selling retail keep Leigh and Bill in contact with the ever changing market. The added time and expense of selling and advertising are paid for by taking the normal retail markup on items sold at *Studio 714.*

● Custom work and repairs to damaged jewelry or antiques build his clientele who return to *Studio 714* to buy his other pieces from time to time. Such custom service develops word-of-mouth advertising that builds retail volume.

● Retail outlets for *Garrison Originals* were picked mainly with one idea in mind,showing jewelry where people with money shop. A gift shop in Colorado, for example, sells to the affluent ski-jet crowd. Gift shops were selected individually mainly from talking with people who knew about them. Bill sells by mail and his approach is to send a sample variety of his handcrafted jewelry to the gift shop for inspection. The handcrafted quality of the *Originals* sells the owner of the shop ordinarily. At first, he allowed the gift shops to sell the *Originals* on consignment—at a 33 per cent commission. But, consignment selling increases his inventory expense and bookkeeping time. When the shops begin selling his items regularly, he offers to sell the jewelry outright at lower wholesale prices. To reduce the shops' risk and to reflect his own confidence, Bill offers to exchange any goods that do not sell for new pieces of equal value.

BUILD YOUR OWN CRAFTS BUSINESS

Craft or talent businesses resemble other businesses in one important sense—volume sales build profits. Unless you learn to produce fast and develop outlets for quantity sales, your craft business will remain small—a hobby or a profitable moon-lighting activity, but not a full-time, fortune-building business. Examine the following volume-building tricks. Then, see page 128 for promotion gimmicks that work.

Handcrafted Pottery

Hand-worked, individually designed coffee mugs, pots for house plants, and brightly glazed tableware are big business today. Nearly every major shopping center includes a "Pot Shop" or equivalent. Potters sell their own creations to the shops in quantity—and the shops offer a wide range of articles from various designer-potters to attract customers. Good management and quantity production are two essentials for a moneymaking craft business, particularly if you are an individual potter. Two different approaches work equally well—

● S—Marketing and Manufacturing incorporated into a fully integrated business of making and selling handcrafted, prestige tableware and pots in volume. The company started with five potters and expanded to nine as soon as the potters could be trained in production methods. Three retail outlets stock an inventory of 1,200 different items in 20 basic lines—from coffee mugs, to tableware sets, to planting pots. Each potter was selected for his experience, talent, and willingness to forego individual recognition. The pieces are sold without the name of the potter attached. Each potter works a minimum of five hours per day, five days a week. During each day, a potter will turn out at least 20 items. Until the products begin to turn over in inventory, the potters take only a minimum fee for their work. To find new outlets, in addition to their own three retail shops, the company exhibits its products at regional gift shows. Interchangeable quality, attention to quantity production, and an emphasis on building volume among many retail outlets keep the business growing and prospering. The S—firm is already laying plans for moving into hand-screened textiles.

● Harriet B—designs, shapes, fires, and sells her own pottery under her own name. To build her reputation, she exhibits at craft shows, enters design competitions, and provides pieces for showing at cooperative craft shops. But, her bread-and-butter money comes from sales to department stores, specialty shops, and gift stores. She has built her reputation by concentrating on individual design until a piece of pottery with her label commands a higher price. Such a reputation takes years to acquire, but Harriet stuck to it. Although she produces quantities of pieces for sale, she continues to concentrate on new designs, unique shapes, distinctive glazes, and an expanded line of products. A key element in her marketing strategy is her twice-yearly "seconds" sale. These items contain minor flaws—outside the scope of handcrafted marks. She advertises her "seconds" sale in local classified sections. So popular are the sales now that customers line up at the door before opening time. Customers carry away armloads of pots and tableware at cut-rate prices. But, note—although the "seconds" sell for a third to a half of prices of similar items in retail stores—Harriet gets as much or more per piece than she does selling wholesale to stores. Ordinarily, stores will not handle goods priced significantly below their own retail prices. But, by billing the sale as a clearance of "seconds," and holding only two sales per year, she converts nearly all of her off-quality products into ready cash. Also, because the demand for her "seconds" has grown so large, she can afford to cull out a larger volume of her production for direct selling. Such culling has another effect—fewer pieces for sale to stores—so, higher prices due to limited supply.

HOW TO TURN YOUR CRAFT-HOBBY INTO A BIG-MONEY BUSINESS

Craft products of all kinds command high individual prices because of their creative design, individuality, and rarity. But eventually sales—and profits—reach a limit because the designer-craftsman simply runs out of time. Spinning off products that can be produced by others can end-run such a road block. Designers and craftsmen can expand markets by—

● Developing and selling equipment for crafts—Baron's cabochon gem polisher grew out of his own desire for a way to polish gemstones in less time and with less fuss. So, his experiments led to an abrasive-faced disk that held diamond dust in paste form for polishing. When visitors and fellow gem polishers wanted to buy one of the polishers for their own use, he began to fabricate the units for sale. Now he does more business assembling and selling the gem polishers than he does selling gemstones. See Chapter 7 for tips on selling such specialized merchandise by mail.

● Selling kits and materials Toddi's "Dipping-Goo" methods for making plastic flowers within looped wires requires little skill and produces colorful, splashy products. But, materials and instructions are so specialized that no regular store carries them. So, Toddi combined everything needed into one convenient package wire, dipping plastic, mounts, and instructions. Like so many synergistic ideas, the package was worth many times the sum of the cost for individual materials. A package that sells for $6.95 plus $1.25 for shipping actually costs less than $1.40 for materials, printed instructions, and packaging. National advertising brings in thousands of orders. No-cost demonstrations and simple classes develop a clientele of amateurs who buy replacement materials over and over again.

●Northwest Products is another example of the profit potential from kit sales. Northwest sells finished wreaths of pine cones, seed pods, and dried miscellany in a range of prices from $6.95 to $195. But, even more profitable than the finished wreaths on a per-hour basis are the bags of cones, leaves, and seed pods sold to amateurs for crafting their own wreaths. Northwest urges amateurs to collect their own pods but collectors invariably buy the rare or unusual pieces to add variety to their wreaths from Northwest—by mail. A small brochure with instructions adds saleability to the package—and the dollars roll in for what many people might consider dried rubbish.

●Teaching classes—Instruction in crafts builds profits two ways—income from students and profits from the sale of equipment and materials. For example, silversmithing and jewelry metal-crafting are so popular, that YMCA's, park and recreation departments, and adult evening schools offer classes in many localities. But, these institutions are seldom equipped to sell tools, equipment, and materials on a continuing basis. So, if you instruct a class, you build a demand for equipment, tools, and materials. You then supply them from your own shop. For example, Dorothy B——began teaching gemstone jewelry making in a local high school. Students paid only $2 each per lesson, but the class attracted 20 students. Dorothy was paid only half of the fee which still netted her $10 per hour for the two-hour class—enough for expenses. Her real payoff came, however, when the students became more skilled—they bought powered equipment. Once a student is hooked on a hobby, he or she will spend hundreds of dollars to equip her shop. A gemstone fancier may start with a $15.95 rock tumbler and graduate to a $395 diamond slabbing and polishing setup.

●Writing articles for local newspapers or national magazines—Payoff from articles in magazines can be enough to cover the time spent, but a bigger payoff comes from the publicity and attention. Rather than try to write your own articles, collaborate with a practicing, selling author—and split any fee down the middle—50 per cent for your projects and know-how—50 per cent for the author's time, drawing, and photographs, if any.

● Writing a complete book on your special craft—Hobby books sell for years and in tremendous quantities. Although royalties usually average about 10 per cent of the selling price, craft books sell from many outlets other than bookstores. *Lapidary Journal,* for example, reports 72,000 books were sold through their associated book department in one year. Writing a book can become a time-consuming project and is no undertaking for an amateur. Collaborate with a professional—and split the royalty 50-50, as with articles. The writer will more than earn his 50-50 split—and you earn the publicity and promotional potential that accrues to a published author. See Promote Your Way to Craft Sales later in this chapter.

BUILD YOUR FORTUNE IN MOTION PICTURES

Documentary motion pictures need not be wide-screen blockbusters to turn a profit for creative writer-cameraman-director-producer teams. Businesses regularly buy training, sales, public relations, and report documentary films. Big companies retain in-house capabilities for producing routine test or research films. But, even these big companies tend to hire creative teams for producing the high-quality films necessary to compete for attention outside their own business. Small production companies operate with a minimum of overhead and a maximum of talent and savvy to serve these markets. You can learn from the example of Dave Gardner and Associates.

Dave learned all phases of motion picture production, from scriptwriting to camerawork—editing to music backgrounds—as head of an in-house motion picture unit. But, the routine quality of research and test reporting scarcely challenged his creative talents. So, when an offer to film a documentary for an outside producer came along, he jumped into independent filming. His big opportunity came along when he was asked to film and edit a travel and recreation promotional film for the State of Washington, narrated by Bing Crosby. The film became a national hit and won awards as the outstanding film of its type. At one time, 156 prints of the film were constantly in motion for showing as short subjects in movie houses, on television, and for group programs both in the U.S. and overseas.

With these credits, Dave teamed up with film writer and photographer Paul Marlow to form Gardner/Marlow Films. The pair continued to produce high-quality special-purpose films. Now they are branching out into educational films, television commercials, and entertainment packages aimed at the burgeoning cable TV market. A hard-headed business approach combined with creative, innovative talent account for the rising star of G/M Films. Some of the lessons Dave Gardner learned the hard way can help you develop your motion picture business—

● Planning for cyclical operations—Up-and-down cycling typically causes problems with film producers of any size—from Metro-Goldwyn-Mayer on down to G/M Films. Individual films may cost from $20,000 to $100,000 and up. As long as three years may elapse from the time an idea germinates until the finished film is delivered, ready for showing. Such planning scarcely proceeds in an orderly, timely fashion. So, a film company may be shooting three films at once—or none. Unless planning and spending allow for the lulls as well as the peaks, film companies disappear during one of the lulls between big jobs. Dave and Paul handle cyclical phasing by—

—Keeping overhead to an absolute minimum. They maintain no staff and no studio. When they need an editor, writer, artist, or sound technician beyond their own capabilities, they hire a moonlighting specialist for a specific job. Much of their shooting takes place on location, but when they need a studio, they rent one by the day from a local television station. The only regular expense is for a small office that doubles as a storeroom for cameras, lighting equipment, and their film library. The office is located out of the high-rent district and satisfies strictly utilitarian functions—no fancy furniture, carpets, or built-in facilities.

—Paying cash for film and processing. A down payment on a film covers such out-of-pocket costs as film, travel expenses, and processing. By paying cash, Dave keeps out of the debt-paying cycle that traps the unwary in the feast-or-famine cycle common in the film business.

—Owning outright the basic camera and lighting equipment used regularly in filming. Dave paid for expensive cameras out of earnings from his first successful film. Now he buys only a few specialized pieces of equipment that he uses repeatedly. He rents unique, highly specialized equipment required for a specific job to keep capital expenditures, low.

—Setting aside money during the busy periods to carry them through the lulls. The tendency to "live it up" when the money from a big job is coming in causes the downfall of less forward-looking producers. Dave and Paul plan for the long pull and retain a kitty to tide them over the inevitable lulls.

● Marketing quality rather than price—Dave does not attempt to compete on price alone and the extra quality pays off in higher profits. With a number of big films to their credit, Dave demonstrates with hard statistics that quality production pays off in more frequent airings on TV and higher bookings for showing to groups. The high price tag for most films forces decisions up to high management levels where quibbling over pennies seldom occurs. Knowledgeable managers usually recognize that quality depends on talent, experience, and know-how—all relatively undefinable in a specification. By holding out for high quality, G/M Films normally brings down 30 per cent of a film's total cost to profit—after paying the partners' salaries.

●With big productions infrequent, Dave schedules the filming of TV commercials to fill in the gaps whenever possible. These bread-and-butter jobs help to take the strain off the savings account during lulls as well as providing a challenge of their own. Working for agencies also keeps creative directors aware of their talents for producing major films. Commercials retain the Dave Gardner quality, but must compete on price. So profit margins suffer. Even so, prices for filming commercials usually cover all costs including minimum salaries plus a contribution to overhead during lulls.

●A not-for-profit subsidiary permits Dave to bid for government grants to film educational projects for the U.S. Dept. of Education. While the subsidiary cannot earn a profit under the incorporation charter, salaries paid to partners are includable as cost along with out-of-pocket expenses for film, travel, and processing, plus that all-important allowance for overhead.

●Speculative filming leads to profits two ways—First, the partners are experimenting with educational films for which they may be the distributor. Rentals and sales of the films to schools and educational TV stations pay for the cost of production plus a profit—if they are good. This program is still largely experimental. But, when time between big jobs hangs heavy, these experimental projects cost little more than the out-of-pocket money for film. Eventually Dave expects educational films to pay more than the price-competitive commercials. Second—for specific companies, where films could become a major marketing media, Dave and Paul consider investing their time in return for shares of stock in the company.

You have one important element going for you in film production. As Dave puts it: "Potential for hitting it really big is always there. Routine productions can net a small company like ours from $20,000 to $50,000 a year—but one of our speculative deals may hit—and we could jump into the $100,000-a-year bracket. We figure we have a better chance of hitting that six-figure profit with quality productions than by trying to make too many films. Our secret, if it really is a secret, is to work like dogs and produce the very best film we're capable of."

HOW TO CASH IN ON HOBBY AND CRAFT SKILLS

You can join that elite group of hobbyists, sportsmen, craftsmen, artists, and talented entrepreneurs who earn big money from their talent by putting your interest, unique know-how, and creative talent to work. Here's how—

Assay Your Skills and Talents

"Thar's gold in them thar hobbies!" But, you have to find the nuggets. Instead of searching haphazardly, try these proven ideas—

● List your skills including *everything* you are reasonably good at or would like to be good at—Interest can lead to skills because motivation pushes aside roadblocks as big as mountains. Boris

H----was always fascinated by player pianos and the ancient mechanical music makers that hammered out tinny tunes before record players and radios. He tinkered, learned how they operated, rebuilt broken parts, replaced worn fabrics and tubing, and put the old-timers back into top operating condition. He soon learned there was a huge market for rebuilt music makers. Today, the Boris H----firm does more than $1 million of sales a year in one-of-a-kind mechanical music machines.

● Place a value on each of your skills—Analyze which of your skills could be turned into a profit-producing business. Develop a plan for each skill, then choose the one which offers the most potential.

Test Your Business by Moonlighting

Develop your productivity, check out prices for products you make, try teaching an evening adult-education class in your hobby or craft, and test a variety of marketing approaches. In developing your moonlighting business, remember these hints—

● Keep your overhead costs low—Students won't object to attending classes in your basement if you fix up benches and supply tools and materials. If you produce products for sale, set up your shop for volume production by designing fixtures and special tools you build yourself.

● Test product profitability—Establish costs for each element of your production, teaching, or sales of equipment and materials. Unless you know your costs down to the penny, you're in no position to go big time.

● Print up a letterhead and business cards—You qualify for wholesale prices on materials, equipment, and parts if you operate a business—and the key is your own business stationery.

● Try various marketing ideas—Test run ads for mail order (see Chapter 7). Exhibit in local craft fairs, art shows, and meetings of craftsmen or hobbyists. Develop markets in gift and novelty shops. Find out as a moonlighter whether you can develop full-time market volume before plunging off the deep end.

Manage Your Business for Profits

Examine every aspect of your part-time business and plan ahead for volume, costs, capital needs, and, most important of all, profits. Remember—you're in business; your activity is no longer a hobby. Too many craft or hobby operators shoot the breeze with customers rather than producing and selling.

TURN YOUR TALENT FOR SPORTS INTO BIG MONEY

Not all talent runs to creative crafts or artistry. A talent for fishing, for example, led Paris M----to develop a completely new line of lead sinkers. Paris considers his creations as truly talent-inspired, and he has the patents to prove their originality. Now, his plant pours more than a ton of lead into tiny molds every week to produce quick-change sinkers that hold their position, even on nylon fishing line. A changeover to automated production is expected to double or triple production—and Paris sells all he can make.

Sailing into the Profit Picture

Sailing know-how and enthusiasm were translated into a growing business by Bob Clark with his Clark Boat Co. For years competitive sailors spent more time sanding, caulking, and painting their wood boats than they did sailing. Bob Clark, an ardent sailor, decided to change all that. After World War II, he learned about making patterns in wood, metal, and glass fiber materials at an Ohio manufacturing plant. He and his wife combined these talents at a new home near Puget Sound's limitless sailing areas.

Clark's first effort was a completely new *Lightning*—a class sailboat built from fiber glass rather than wood. Although the first copies from his hull mold set no records in competition, it immediately caught on because of its low maintenance. With less time in the shop, boats could spend more time on the water in competition. Although advertisements in boating magazines caught a few sailors' attention—the sleek, unsinkable hulls were their best advertisement when the Clark clan raced at regattas. Orders began flowing in. Then, Clark added a mold for building sailing dinghies and for building the ski-rescue sleds used at nearby winter skiing resorts.

But, the boat that really caught on came from the creative experience of father Bob and son Don, a budding naval architect. Dubbed the *C-Lark*, the 14-foot sailboat featured a whopping 133 square feet of sail, a self-bailing cockpit when stored either in the water or pulled up on a float, and cast-in color for minimum maintenance. The large jib and mainsail could be further extended with a spinnaker for competition. The *C-Lark* offered real competitive qualities for a skipper plus crewman or a skipper alone. The *C-Larks* trailered easily to regattas and featured a lightweight aluminum mast for quick stepping and unstepping. The sailboat was light enough for two adults to move up or off a float. *C-Larks* immediately caught on, with the help of Mrs. Clark and her *C-Lark* Association. The Clark Boat Co. recently moved into a new building that will permit doubled production rates and lower costs through improved efficiency. The full line of fiber glass boats includes the *Lightning, C-Lark, Thistle, O.K. Dinghy, Geary-18, San Juan 21, Tadpole, Star, and International 14.* Although Bob Clark combined an enthusiasm for sailing with a talent for hull designing and no-nonsense skills of pattern making and glass fiber plastic layup techniques, you can learn from these other factors that built a solid success for the Clark Boat Co.—

● *Lightnings* constructed of glass-fiber reinforced plastic attracted immediate attention among the 9,000-plus *Lightning* owners because Bob and his family raced in regattas. Other sailors couldn't help but notice the clean lines of the glass-fiber hull. They mentally pictured the sharply reduced upkeep labor and expense. The *C-Lark* caught on quickly because it fulfilled a need for a smaller, fully competitive boat operable by two—or a skipper alone.

● Clark built boats only on order. *Lightnings* originally started at $2,150—more than comparable wood hulls at the time. Prices have risen only modestly but costs have declined due to production efficiency. Smaller *C-Larks* were produced on order and for sale directly and through marinas. However, most customers preferred to buy their boats directly from the factory—and trailer them home.

● Clark seldom borrowed money, preferring to plow back any cash flow into the business and grow only as rapidly as profits permitted. At the beginning, the family lived mainly on Mrs. Clark's earnings as a nurse. The three Clark boys pitched in to build the boats. And Mrs. Clark kept books as well as keeping house.

●Marketing relied heavily on actual sailing in competitive regattas. The Clarks hauled their *Lightnings* all over the Pacific Northwest, competed in races at every opportunity, and talked with sailors wherever they could find them. When the *C-Lark* was available in number, Mrs. Clark started the *C-Lark* Association, promoted races, encouraged clubs to sponsor regattas, and used the publicity to spread the word about their new one-class racing hulls.

PROMOTE YOUR WAY TO CRAFT SALES

Getting people to know you and about your products or services for sale takes (1) money and/or (2) imagination. Since you are talented and creative, exploit these imaginative ways to promote your business—for little or no cost.

Exhibit at Arts and Crafts Fairs

People flood to these two- to five-day exhibits as a holiday or educational experience. They also buy hundreds of dollars worth of your craft products. Follow these hints for increasing your visibility and sales—

●Keep active—Provide a show by carving decorative panels, forging and soldering jewelry, painting, or shaping projects. Activity draws a crowd—and crowds become buyers.

●Promote impulse items—Crafts that sell for 25 cents to $5.00 will attract buyers when $300-$600 paintings or jewelry won't sell.

●Hand out low-key folders to remind strollers where they can find you when the show is over—for craft projects, lessons, or materials. These are the buyers who will pick up your expensive pieces.

●Enter competition—Do this mainly to promote your name on a program or list of winners in the judging.

●Test new ideas, products, and designs on visitors. Shows offer unparalleled chances to test the public's interest in your crafts.

Encourage Print Publicity

An article in the Sunday magazine section of your news-paper can be worth thousands of dollars. A two-page article describing a new creative writing school started by John and Marilyn Housbeck brought in more registrations than they could handle—so they started a waiting list. Here's how you get publicity—

●Write up a straightforward, factual article about your craft or hobby. Keep "selling" copy to a minimum; concentrate instead on anything new about your activity—methods, design, unusual materials, prizes won—something out of the ordinary to catch an editor's interest. If you absolutely cannot write such an article, barter with one of your writer friends to do the job.

●Hire a photographer to shoot a series of professional pictures. Snapshots with your "Brownie" won't do. Here again, barter with the photographer by trading your craft projects for finished 8 x 10 glossy photos. Concentrate on action plus close-ups of your best work.

●Contact your Sunday magazine section editor personally. Usually he (often a she) is searching for human-interest articles like yours. If that doesn't work, examine the newspaper for feature writers who by-line their columns or articles and contact one of them. Don't give up. If you have a choice of newspapers, try them all—the one with the biggest circulation first. If the big dailies don't bite—move on to the weekly shoppers. If the weekly papers won't bite, try your organization newsletters. Any start is better than none.

●Offer to supply photos and working drawings of certain projects to a free-lance writer for development into an article for a national magazine. Vashon Industries achieved national attention when *Popular Mechanics* ran an article on their model rockets (see Chapter 7).

Personalize Your Activities

You and your craft or hobby business can interest viewers of a local television station. You can volunteer to talk and show colored slides before groups of all kinds—church circles, PTA groups, library meetings, lodge programs—anywhere people meet and need a no-cost program. Often an article in your newspaper leads to invitations to appear on television, usually on one of the local talk shows. Here you bring samples of your work and talk about how you started, anecdotes, problems, and, as a plug, where your viewers can buy your products. Try the direct approach; send one of the local stations some samples of your work and a brief write-up about your activities.

Program chairmen of organizations are your contacts for lectures. Of course, you don't charge for these program appearances. You talk in exchange for the publicity from those who attend plus the written notice mailed to members. Publicity has a cumulative effect—each little bit adds to the total and makes the next step that much easier. For example, you may not get a nibble from a TV producer until articles have appeared about you in the newspaper, a book you have written is published, or you have appeared on numerous programs around your city. Soon you become a celebrity of sorts. And all that beautiful, free publicity helps you expand your craft or hobby business.

7

Mail-Order Selling--
Your Key to Home-Base Profits

Few small businesses offer the full United States—even the world—as a source of orders, but mail-order depends on a wide clientele. Here you learn the success secrets pioneered by mail-order operators who literally coin money from their mailbox. These proven methods for mail-order profits include—

- *Starting a moonlight operation as a test of your ideas.*
- *Selecting a product line that's best merchandised by mail because of its appeal to a dilute market and its unusual, specialized nature.*
- *Recognizing the different kinds of costs involved— mainly the cost of "buying orders."*
- *Advertising and promoting your products for low cost and high returns.*
- *Keeping a sharp watch on costs.*
- *Satisfying mail-order clients to build repeat business.*
- *Working amicably with the post office—your real-life place of business.*

TV advertisements of Vashon Industries' *Valkyrie* during the fabulous moon walks of Apollo swamped the fledgling firm with orders. The liquid-fueled *Valkyrie* rockets attain altitudes of more than 1,000 feet and are advertised as safe and reliable. At its maximum height, the rocket deploys its own parachute to return it to ground safely. The firm started out in a garage on Vashon Island near Seattle and sold its first model rockets entirely by mail through ads in *Boys Life, Jr. Scholastic,* and *Model Rocketry* magazines. Complete rockets sell for under $15. Now Vashon Industries employs 25 people and can supply 10,000 rocket kits every month.

Another million-dollar entrepreneur started his own mail-order selling business by shipping out orders from his basement. He and his wife opened envelopes, filled the orders, hauled station-wagon loads of packages to the post office every day, and deposited the cash daily in the bank. For a full year, just the two of them built the business until volume became too large for them to handle out of their basement. Now, the mail-order retailer sells millions of dollars worth of goods every year.

Another mail-order businessman tried marketing kits of wood projects for Cub Scouts and groups of children. In order to attract buyers, he dropped his price in steps from 79 cents per kit to 29 cents per kit. But, although the volume of orders increased as prices dropped, his margin for profit and overhead went down even faster. While the 29-cent price covered materials and a small return for each hour of labor he put in, there was no money left to pay for advertising. So, his business folded—for two reasons: (1) unit price was too low for economic handling; and (2) product, pieces of wood cut to fit into a simple-to-build project, was not unique and failed to offer something that was either not available locally or could not easily be made by a craftsman.

YOUR GUIDE TO SUCCESSFUL
MAIL-ORDER OPERATIONS

Mail order selling calls for a highly specialized form of marketing. You must persuade customers who have never had the chance to meet you, to examine your products or the service you provide, to place orders with you. You must overcome reluctance to take action and must create an atmosphere of confidence that you will deliver satisfactorily. Thousands of people, however, have succeeded in achieving these goals. The mail order business continues to expand as a healthy segment in marketing, with these unique features—

●Independent location—Your office can be anywhere near a post office. You can operate out of a spare bedroom, your basement, or a garage. Mail-order addresses can be and are nearly anywhere. But, since supplies and goods must be shipped in, locations near transportation centers offer quick access to suppliers.

●Ideal for moonlighting—Few business opportunities afford the easy-start possibilities of mail-order selling. Overhead can be low if you operate from your home. Even if zoning normally restricts your area to nonbusiness activities, a mail-order business in your basement seldom draws a complaint. Mail-order selling starts slowly, so you build the business in your spare time and add help only as volume demands. By working at a paying job, you need not depend on mail-order income for living expenses—so mistakes in judgment won't force you out of business at the beginning. Packaging and order handling can be split off to family members to keep start-up costs low. Routine envelope opening, order picking, packaging, and mailing are easily handled by boys and girls in junior high grades and older. Because orders come in and out by mail, you schedule time when it is available—not by rigid store hours or at customers' convenience.

●Expanding opportunities—Mail-order businesses are on the rise and opportunities open as fast as logical-thinking entrepreneurs can develop them. Merchandising by mail is growing faster than any branch of marketing, with sales in excess of $25 billion a year. Even though Sears, Wards, and Spiegels satisfy half of that dollar volume, $12.5 billion offers a lot of operating room for the newcomer. Main reasons behind the booming mail-order business include—

—People have more money to spend, particularly for hobbies and fun. So, mail-order firms supplying everything from rockhound supplies to fur-lined parkas sell to a thin, widely dispersed clientele by mail. Why by mail rather than from a store? Because the demand for specialty goods (diamond saws, hunting bows, and the like) comes from the whole United States and foreign countries rather than a specific city. Stores can stock the wide variety necessary to cater to specialty tastes only if they can tap a countrywide market. So, a specialty supplier, like Recreational Equipment, Inc., sells mountain-climbing equipment from its huge Seattle store and offers its full line all over the world through its colorful catalog.

—Many busy people would rather shop from a catalog than travel to a big shopping center, fight traffic, and stand in line at counters.

—Goods available by mail are described in catalogues in great detail, enabling buyers to compare specifications closely and precisely instead of relying on clerks who know little about the products they sell.

—Tastes in goods of every description are splintering into so many directions, that volume in specialties comes only by tapping a wider market than is available to walk-in customers.

● Mail-order businesses depend on the unusual and the unique. Examine the advertisements in a typical magazine's mail-order section. You'll find products and services highlighting the unique and the unusual, such as—

—Novelties—Colorful catalogs offer everything from monogrammed scissors to giant forks, kitchen aids, and gimmicks. Imaginative developments, imports, and personalized or monogrammed products with initials or full names fill the gay catalogs—but would seldom pay for counter space in a store due to the dilute market.

—Clothes for distinction or sports—Hunting boots, rain

gear, down-filled parkas, wool shirts and jackets, and imports with old-world trade names offer quality and functional distinction not available from local stores. Prices on specialty clothing run up to 20 per cent higher than similar goods purchased in stores. But, stores either do not handle the specialty clothes or the quality is low. Specialty suppliers, like Eddie Bauer, Recreational Equipment, Norm Thompson, and L. L. Bean offer top-quality goods for the sportsman or individual who wants something unique—and is willing to pay for it.

—Sporting goods—Fishing equipment, hunting boots and camping gear, and guns or fishing rods are big business—and becoming more specialized every year. Specialization and unique products usually spell low volume—so marketing depends heavily on mail order in addition to a major store that also serves as a stock room and shipping facility.

—Electronic and mechanical supplies—Few stores can stock even a fraction of the parts and assemblies needed to supply radio and electronic experimenters, auto modifiers, or repair shops. So, Allied Radio stocks practically everything an electronics or laboratory builder could want, J.C. Whitney & Co. stocks automotive accessories and parts for all domestic and imported cars, and Heathkit supplies electronic kits to satisfy nearly every taste.

—Hobby supplies—Stamp sets, old or rare coins, stitchery kits, specialty supplies, and unique gemstones all reach individuals by mail.

—Gardening materials—Everything from packets of seeds to shrubs are sold by mail, despite equal quality but more limited selection at lower prices from local stores. Mail-order plants and seeds offer something unique—new hybrids, patented roses, or newly developed tomato seeds—so mail-order selling to gardeners everywhere yields profits.

—Correspondence instruction—Schools offering instruction by mail range from the volume operations of university extension divisions to a specialized school of stitchery—and include the big schools that teach trade and job skills.

—Food specialties—Cheese, freeze-dried food specialties for backpacking campers, luscious steaks from corn-country butchers, and imported delicacies all share one unique quality—they're expensive. But, such suppliers obviously supply a need for gift or unusual foods not locally available.

—Surplus dealers—Government surplus, everything from trench shovels to special vehicles, are purchased on bid from sales by the Department of Defense and sold through ads for special items or catalogs of a wide variety of goods by mail. Surplus dealers are one of the few mail-order sellers that emphasize low prices. The other group of low-price sellers promote special imports such as cameras, tape recorders, etc., for sale directly through the mails.

An examination of the products and services ᴖffered yields at least two overriding conclusions: (1) prices on specialty goods usually range higher than for similar goods purchased in stores (except for surplus and import sales); (2) mail-order selling caters to highly specialized groups (except novelty sales where the appeal is personal or through variety). Other conclusions—

● Mail-order businesses fail more often than any other broad category of business. Statistics indicate that nine out of ten mail-order businesses fail within one year. Firms that survive usually start small and build with successful experience. You'll find the success-building factors extracted from this experience later in this chapter.

● Mail-order success has been oversold as a quick, no-work road to riches. Not so, according to those who know best—the successful mail-order operators. Mail-order selling can be extremely profitable—but success depends on finding the right product or service, marketing it aggressively, and hard work.

● Costs of acquiring business, mainly advertising and catalogs, offset other low overhead costs. Unless advertising is professionally done with an eye to costs and returns, the business fails for lack of business volume. See page 141 for details on how to measure advertising results and successful tips for maximizing advertising results.

● Long lag between investment and profit for most mail-order businesses demands a long-pull approach and patience when getting started. Advertising itself builds in a lag because ads must be placed one to three months ahead of publication. Then, inquiries must be answered or catalogs mailed. After another wait, orders may come in. From four to six months may have elapsed before you know if you have a winner or not. You can shorten response cycles by using mailing lists and direct-mail advertising. Direct mail may be more expensive on a per-order basis than periodical advertising—but not necessarily. See page 143 for details on direct-mail selling.

Far East Silks is only one example of a successful mail-order business. *Far East* sells exotic dress and sewing yard goods by mail to home seamstresses. In one year the firm filled 12,000 orders ranging from $5 to more than $100 each, with an average in the $15-$20 range. Note the following specific points that contribute to *Far East's* success—

● Specialization—Far East sells only imported, high-quality silk and long-staple cotton materials in bright, Oriental colors. Variety in colors and patterns greatly exceeds the limited showing of similar materials in local dress goods shops. So, it specialized and offers something not available in wide variety locally.

● Prices—Through volume selling of a limited line of goods, Far East sells for about 75-80 per cent of normal retail prices for similar dress goods in local stores. So, home seamstresses can buy from a greater selection at lower prices—a double appeal. Since home dressmakers usually tailor their own clothes to save money, low prices appeal to their thrifty natures.

● Advertising—*Far East* places specialized ads in magazines that pre-select readers obviously interested in home sewing. *Vogue Pattern Book* and *McCall's Needlework and Crafts* are read mainly by women who tailor their own clothes. So, ads appeal directly to prospects' known interests. *Far East* also maintains its own mailing list for repeated offerings to previous customers or inquirers.

● Sample fabrics—Rather than pay for large color ads to display the brilliant colors of the exotic silks, *Far East* uses many small ads in a variety of magazines and offers swatches of actual fabrics for $3 a bunch. Women like to examine actual colors and feel texture rather than buy from pictures. But, selling sample swatches pays poorly. Since the main idea is to sell yard goods from swatches, *Far East* refunds the full cost of samples or credits their cost on an order when the sample swatches are returned. But, most home sewers retain the samples anyway for future orders. Sample swatches are small 2" x 2" chunks cut from bolt ends or scraps. Selections are simply stapled together with identifying numbers to simplify ordering.

● Service—Quick filling of orders caters to home sewers' interest in getting started quickly. Cut lengths of fabrics are shipped in an envelope by Special Handling (first-class speed), so that orders are received within three to five days after an order is mailed.

● Repeat business—Price and quality of *Far East* fabrics generate repeat orders among satisfied purchasers. Home sewers also pass sample swatches around among friends, so that volume sales build with time.

● Expansion—*Far East* offers beaded sweaters (high labor content for individually sewn beads through low-cost labor in Hong Kong and Thailand), handbags, fiber products, and the like—all imported from the Orient—through special mailings to its list of customers. Beautifully printed color circulars bring these follow-on products to *Far East* customers at a fraction of the cost because, along with exotic fabrics, *Far East* buys color printing in Hong Kong.

YOUR STEP-BY-STEP GUIDE TO A MAIL-ORDER BUSINESS OF YOUR OWN

You can develop your own profitable business and avoid the traps that cause failures by following these steps in turn—

Select a Product Uniquely Marketable by Mail

Most important for successful mail-order operation is a product or service that stands out from the usual, a product that appeals to specialized interests, and one that is not generally available in stores because of the thin market. For example, *Far East Silks* trades on variety and authenticity—silks imported from Thailand, Hong Kong, and India. Few stores carry more than a few bolts of such fabrics. So, *Far East* offers unique colors and textures. *Craftsman Wood Service* stocks exotic hardwoods, such as zebrawood, rosewood, and others, along with special woodworking tools for craftsmen. Such hardwoods simply are not available in lumber yards.

● Avoid costly goods. Items that cost more than $25 are hard to sell until you have established a big business. Costly goods require an expensive inventory, and most people like to see and examine goods before they spend important money on them.

● Sell a product that interests you, particularly if you have developed an invention, can provide a one-of-a-kind service, or sell products you make yourself. Mail-order provides an excellent outlet for crafts and hobby products.

● Examine magazines like *Lapidary Journal, Popular Mechanics, McCall's Needlework and Crafts,* and others with large mail-order advertising to see the kind of products and services offered. *Lapidary Journal,* for example, carries ads for products and services of interest to rockhounds and jewelry craftsmen. Advertisers sell through catalogs or direct from advertised lists of products. Books too specialized for sale through most bookstores sell readily by mail. You can get an idea of the kind of products that sell by studying what successful mail-order entrepreneurs are currently selling.

Develop Your Plan After Study and Trial

Aside from the many books written about mail-order selling, you'll find no specific training available. Your best bet is to follow these proven steps for getting started with the least risk—

● Study and analyze your market according to your product or service. Your analysis should include prices at which comparable products are sold in stores and through the mail, who and where your competitors are, where you expect to find your customers, and some ideas about how to contact potential buyers. Unless you have invented some unique product, you can expect to compete with others already in the marketplace. Your job—find an appeal that will attract orders.

● Start small and build volume as you learn. Pricing, handling and filling orders, advertising and/or direct mail, plus inventory investment must all be balanced with your learning. You can expect to make mistakes—so start small so you can survive your mistakes.

● Develop a profit plan before you spend penny No. 1. As part of your study and analysis, you should know—not guess at—prices you will pay for goods, time required for handling, mailing costs, some estimate of advertising expense, and an estimate of sales volume. Don't expect to be 100 per cent right. But, setting a plan down on paper requires you to think about every item of your business. For example, suppose your plan for selling handcrafted jewelry kits looks like entries in Table 7A. Note the allowance for handling inquiries because not every customer will buy directly from an ad—even with a coupon. The important elements are advertising expense, your cost for assembling the kits (including the price of the materials, package, printed instructions, and wages), a price for your time, postage and wrapping, and a profit. Note that profit accrues in addition to your allowance for wages. You must estimate some volume of business—and volume can easily be 100 per cent higher or 80 per cent lower than your estimate. All the more reason to start small, so you can estimate volume closely before expanding.

Table 7A

START-UP PROFIT PLAN -- 1,000 Units

Jewelry Handcrafted Kits—	
@1.50 each	$1,500
1,000 Inquiry Answers	
Includes printing and postage - 20¢ each	
for materials plus 20¢ handling	400
Postage, boxes, and wrapping - 40¢ each	400
Wages for handling	500
Cost of Goods Sold	$2,800
Advertising	$1,800
Profit	$350
Total Estimated Sales	$4,950

Operate Professionally

Nothing turns off a mail-order buyer as quickly as evidence that he is dealing with an amateur. So, play the game like an expert. For example—

- Print your letterheads, envelopes, shipping labels, and order blanks. Fortunately, instant printing services provide professional-quality printing at low cost for short runs as long as you don't use photographs. Seek out one of the quick-printing firms and ask them for a lead to a cold-typesetting shop where you can buy layout and type for a fraction of the cost charged by big printing houses.

- Develop a unique graphics symbol or image—called a LOGO. Use the LOGO on your letterheads and in your advertisements for instant identity. A moonlighting artist can develop a symbol that identifies your firm and/or your product.

- Organize a handling system to get orders in the mail quickly—preferably within 24 hours of receiving an order. If an order will be delayed for any reason—parts not in stock, order desk swamped with business—*anything*—send a post card advising the customer that his order has been received and will be shipped by----------, an estimated date. Remember, parcel-post delivery sometimes takes as long as two to four weeks.

- Use printed handling forms to simplify paper work. Sales slips, order lists, invoices, credit forms—the works. Depending on your product, you will need a variety of these internal pieces of paper. Unless you plan operations for quick, efficient handling, you will spend too much time—and you will earn less pay for your time than you expected. Or, if you hire outside help to process orders and inquiries, the cost will reduce profits unless your plan for handling eliminates every unnecessary step. Check with your accountant for the minimum number of records necessary to keep books for tax and internal reporting.

Advertising and Promotion

Mail-order business depends on attracting customers through advertising, direct mail, or promotion. Unless you plan your campaigns with an eye to immediate response, you will have spent your money and gained few orders. Follow these proven tips for developing mail-order sales—

● Use classified advertisements for low-cost trials while you start small. Classified ads enable you to try different appeals until you find the one that brings in hundreds of orders or inquiries. Only then should you move into space ads. Experiment with different magazines, different approaches (make more money or enjoy your hobby), and with different prices if your product or service permits.

● Write long copy—in other words, tell everything you believe a potential buyer MUST know before he sends in an order—without wasting a word—because words in classified ads may cost from 40 cents to $15 each.

● Key your ads so you know exactly where every order originates. Easy keys to your ads, either classified or display, are by—

—Changing your street address or P.O. Box number slightly without affecting your delivery. For example, your address is 3344A East Pacific for one magazine, 3344B for another. Avoid using E, W, N, or S or any combination like NE that might confuse the postman. For a box number, add a letter, as P.O. Box 1701-A

—Changing your company name slightly, again without affecting postal delivery. If your firm name is Pacific Trading Company, use Pacific Trade Company in one magazine, Pacific Trading Co., in another, Pacific Trade Co., in a third, or Pacific Trading Cy. in a fourth, and so on. Combine address and company name changes to get many different keys,

—Adding Dept. C or Desk H is an obsolete method of keying and should be avoided. Most customers will simply delete such additions and you cannot identify the source.

—Using coupons with the key printed on the return form display space. Instead of a coupon, try offering a small premium if they return the whole ad with an order.

● Calculate your advertising costs closely before and after results are in. For example, with magazines you figure ad cost per thousand circulation. Most magazines belong to the Audit Bureau of Circulation, ABC, which guarantees circulation figures. Divide your cost for an ad by the circulation in thousands to get your cost per thousand. You'll find that—

—Cost per thousand falls as circulation increases. An ad may cost 43 cents per thousand in a magazine with 46,000 circulation and only 12 cents per thousand in a magazine with 4 million circulation. But, the dollar cost of the ad may be $20 in the first and $480 in the second. When beginning, watch total dollar cost as well as cost per thousand.

—Cost per thousand will be higher in specialized magazines than in general magazines. Specialized magazines sell preselected readership through their editorial approach—so your ad reaches fewer noninterested readers. Specialized magazines, generally, are better suited to mail-order advertising because of this preselected readership. *Model Rocketry,* for example, is highly selective for Vashon Industries, compared to *Popular Mechanics'* more general though vastly larger readership.

—Cost per order, figured after all orders are in or on a monthly basis for continuing ads, signal the real payoff. When advertising, you are "buying orders." So, aim to buy orders for the least possible expense consistent with the volume you expect to fulfill your plan. For example, you can buy a few orders inexpensively with small classified advertisements in selected magazines. But, to expand your sales volume, you may need to advertise in other magazines or go into display (space) ads—with an increase in cost per order. Keep exact records of your returns and cost per order to plan future ads. You will find, after experiments, that you get more for your advertising dollars in certain magazines, newspapers, or on radio than others. You may find that direct mail produces more orders per dollar than advertising.

● Offer leaders, premiums, or bonuses to pull orders. Contests or "you may have already won a prize" promotions pull inquiries and orders. No-profit leaders, much like the advertised specials by grocers, provide another appeal. Premiums, such as a folder on "Where to Sell Jewelry," or a bonus of an extra kit of materials for prompt payment, keep communications open and attract buyers who look for that something extra. Premiums and bonuses work better than price cuts, because you can discontinue the premium later without affecting the basic price of your offerings.

● Try direct mail for two reasons—quick response and testing sales letters. Magazine advertising requires months to find answers to ads because of the lead time for placing ads and the wait for results.

With direct mail, you send out a mailing and within two to three weeks you know the results. On a cost-per-thousand basis, direct mail can be double, triple, or more than the costs of magazine advertising. You must rent the names, prepare sales literature, and pay postage for each mailing. However, you can include much more information (long copy) in direct mailing and your list of names can be highly selective. Split mailings offer a chance to experiment on ad copy and reader appeal. With a split mailing, you prepare two sets of selling copy, each with a different appeal. When you send the copy to a mailer, specify that odd-numbered names get one set and even names get the second set. A coupon or return envelope in each packet keys your response. So, if you get three times as many returns from Set A as you do from Set B, you KNOW, rather than guess, which appeal exerts the most pulling power. The Small Business Administration publishes *National Mailing-List Houses,* Bibliography No. 29, which lists the major suppliers of mailing lists. The more selective a list is, the greater the cost per name. To rent a list, you send your sales literature along with postage to a mailer who attaches the names and addresses and mails them. Check your yellow pages for local mailers with access to national mailing lists.

For further information, check these books: *Successful Direct -Mail Advertising and Selling,* Robert Stone, Prentice-Hall, Inc. *Measuring Advertising Results,* Darrel Blaine Lucas and Stewart Henderson Britt, Mc Graw-Hill, Inc., New York, N.Y..*How to Make More Money with Your Direct Mail,* Edward N. Mayer, Jr. Marketing/Communications, New York, N.Y.

Learn to Work with Your Post Office

Your mail-order business depends absolutely on the post office. Learn everything there is to know about mailing, service, and the small items that can help your business. For example, by printing the words RETURN REQUESTED on a package, the post office will return undelivered third- or fourth-class mail for a fee. This way you keep your mailing list up-to-date and/or retrieve merchandise you would otherwise lose. First-class mail costs so much per ounce, but undelivered mail is returned automatically. Second-class privileges are not normally available to mail-order operators. However, there are at least three ways to use third-class mail, plus special services such as Special Handling, which speeds fourth-class mail at the same rate as first-class mail.

Ask your local post office for its free circulars on various kinds of mail. *Mailing Permits* is a circular that tells about business return permits (they cost you nothing) and the current fees for bulk and precancelled third-class mailings. Since these rules and prices change regularly, your best bet is to check with your postmaster for rules and prices that will affect you.

One final hint–operate your mail-order business on a "satisfaction guaranteed or your money back" basis. You'll get full cooperation from the post office–plus you will build confidence among your potential mail-order customers.

8

Franchising--Your Odds-On Bet to Earn Your Fortune

Management skills and access to capital account for the success of more small businesses than all other factors combined. Franchising adds one more powerful factor —individual motivation—to the package. As a result, franchising is expanding at an explosive pace with no limit in sight. Your chances of success in a franchised business can be eight times higher than if you start on your own because franchising—

- *Offers management systems, tested and refined through experience at many locations.*
- *Sells known products, many nationally promoted, to build brand loyalty and to attract attention.*
- *Offers both operating and capital-gain profits, depending on which kind of franchise you might select.*
- *Matches your interests to an existing, successful system.*
- *Allows you easy access to capital because of the proven success of nationally known franchisers and their professional aid.*

Would you like to improve the odds of success in your own business by as much as eight to one? Then consider franchising. No element of our economy appears to be growing faster than the franchising industry. You've seen the *Dairy Queens, McDonald's,* and *Chicken Delight* businesses mushroom around the country the past few years. These fast-food outlets represent only one group of franchises. Automobile sales agencies, service stations by the major oil companies, and the motel chains are long-standing forms of franchised operations. New ones pop up every day, it seems. One of them could be your ticket to a business of your own.

Franchising is big business—more than 1,000 companies sell franchises as they expand operations. More than 600,000 franchisees currently are operating, and new ones are joining the field at a rate of 40,000 per year. Franchises contribute about 10 per cent to the gross national product. One estimate indicates that about 25 per cent of all retail sales in the U.S. are made by franchised operators.

WHAT IS FRANCHISING?

Franchising is one form of licensing by which the owner (franchiser) of a product, service, or method obtains distribution at the retail level through affiliated dealers (franchisees). Two primary factors are present in franchising—

● A legal or contractual relationship that binds the franchiser and the franchisee together, clearly spelling out the obligations and responsibilities of each party.

● A strong, continuing relationship between the franchiser and franchisee for such activities as management assistance and training, merchandising aids, and purchasing assistance. At the beginning, the franchiser also provides a number of other services, such as site selection, market surveys, architectural design of buildings, business training, financial help, and others, depending on the nature of the franchise.

WHY DOES FRANCHISING WORK?

Any industry that is booming, as franchising is booming, must have something going for it. As a budding businessman, consider these pluses and minuses—

- Minimum risk—By trading on the franchiser's experience and management know-how, you begin well down the learning curve. The franchiser has already made most of the mistakes, and you benefit from his corrections and proven results. Records indicate franchised operators fail only about one-eighth as often as independent operators. So, although a franchise does not guarantee success, your odds improve by a factor of eight to one.

- Established product—As a franchisee of one of the big fast-food outlets, like *McDonald's* or *Kentucky Fried Chicken,* you market a product already well-known and accepted. Many franchisers advertise nationally to build business volume for all of their franchisees. You benefit because national promotion brings customers to your store.

- Proven operating methods—Part of the package you buy along with the franchise is start-up help and continuing aid in financing, accounting, analysis of operations, on-the-job management training, and, often, a book of procedures that details every part of the operation.

- Reduced independence—Although you put up all or most of the money required, you must recognize that, as a franchisee, your freedom of operation may be limited. A franchiser may insist that you operate your business strictly according to his rules and procedures. Otherwise, he will cancel your franchise. So, you can't operate strictly as your own boss. The franchiser lays down rules of operation for two reasons—

> 1. Every franchisee depends on the goodwill built up by all the other franchisees. A customer who gets a poor hamburger in New Jersey or Florida may stay away from your place. You must maintain standards of appearance, product quality, and uniform operations to protect all franchises including your own. Your options and flexibility may be strictly limited if you buy into certain franchise chains, and you should check out these conditions before signing.

2. Franchisers work diligently to keep you from failing, because both you and he lose if your franchise fails. So, a franchiser insists that you follow methods and procedures he knows have worked elsewhere. Some of the options you may give up as a franchisee include—

—Which products you will sell and the price at which you will sell them.

—Hours and days of business you will stay open.

—Design of your shop. Nationwide identity for many franchise companies calls for a standard design for your building, sign, and other graphic symbols.

—Identification of your name with the business. The name of the franchiser's product brings in more customers than your name on the outlet. So, you may have to give up the ego boost of putting your name on the marquee.

● Added cost—Considerable controversy surrounds the element of franchise fees and royalties. When you buy a franchise, you pay an initial fee for goodwill, a trademark, training, and management know-how. Franchise contracts also call for a variety of continuing charges—a percentage of gross sales, purchases of specific goods from the parent company at a standard price, management fees, advertising assessments, and others. Whether a business costs more to operate as a franchise than independently requires a detailed analysis of each business. But, overall, despite the higher initial fees, you will usually benefit as a franchisee from lowered interest rates on borrowed money, better chances for success, and reduced costs of materials and/or products through mass purchasing. As the size of a business increases, so does your advantage of operating as a franchisee rather than independently.

Franchisers must also benefit—and they do. Just a few of the reasons companies license franchisees to use their methods and sell their products are—

●Individual management—When a company grants you a franchise to operate one or more outlets for its products or services, the company buys your motivated self-interest to succeed and make money for yourself. If you operate the franchise like your very own business, you spend whatever time it takes to keep it running. You make decisions as a manager—not as an employee. With your profits squarely on the line, you respond like a member of the company's management. So, franchiser management overhead can be cut to a minimum.

● Expanded financing—When you put up all or most of the money to open a franchised business, you effectively expand the financial resources of the parent company. So, a franchiser expands his sales with a minimum investment of his own capital. The franchiser may aid you in financing your business, but he usually lends only his credit rating to help you get a loan.

● Community acceptance—With you running a franchised business, the franchiser trades on your relationships as a member of the local community.

● Rapid expansion—You and other franchisees join in partnership (through a detailed contract, to be sure) with the franchiser. Expansion through franchising allows a franchiser to open many branch offices or sales outlets with a minimum of risk.

Reduced Failure Rate

A major attraction of franchising revolves around the sharply lower failure rate of franchisees compared to independent businessmen. Statistics vary depending on the definition of failure—a loss of 30-40 per cent of the investment (in a turnover), bankruptcy, or closure to stop loss constitute criteria of financial failure. Other failures may result from a variety of personal reasons. The failure rate for franchises may average around 8 to 10 per cent after ten years, compared to a failure of around 80 per cent for stores and other small independent businesses. Capitalization affects the failure rate, with failures of firms with more than $100,000 initial capital, averaging less than 10 per cent, compared to a failure rate of around 80 per cent (after ten years) for companies that start with $5,000 or less initial investment. Several reasons account for the difference: More capital breeds success by itself. Managers able to raise more money to start are usually more capable than managers who start with minimum capital. Businesses requiring large outlays of capital to start enjoy less competition because of the difficulties of entry.

WHICH KIND OF FRANCHISE FOR YOU?

Franchising has expanded so broadly that a variety of franchise opportunities are diverging into recognized specialties. Make sure you know which one you may be interested in.

Operating Franchise

Most common is the single-outlet franchise where you buy the rights to open a retail store or service facility as part of a franchise chain. A single *A to Z Rental Center* is one outlet. Usually, you are protected from someone else opening another franchise operation by that franchiser in your natural trading territory—but, you are not protected from a competitor from another chain opening a shop much like yours in the next block.

Multiple-Unit Franchises

Rather than being limited to only one operating unit, your franchise agreement may permit you to open and operate more than one unit if the volume and the territory will support them. You become a manager of several units, but the franchise remains yours within a specified geographical territory.

Operating Franchises with Sub-Licensing

In addition to operating one or more units under your own franchise agreement, you are permitted to sub-license other independent franchisees to open similar units. You may be granted such wide-ranging authority over a state or a multi-state area. You must not only operate your own units consistent with franchise standards, but you must supervise anyone you sub-license. You earn a manager's fee on the operations of all the units you sub-license plus a portion of the usual initial fee.

Area Franchises

Rather than operate even one unit, you buy a franchise for

a specified area that permits you to license operators. You recruit, train, and supervise their operations in accordance with methods and procedures developed by the franchiser. As an area franchisee, you operate as a part of the franchiser's management team, but your earnings reflect the number of operating franchises you establish and their profitability.

Franchise for Marketing Franchises

So bewildering is the variety of franchises now available, you may get confused in trying to find the ONE franchise best for you. One aid in this search is the franchise agent. He represents a number of franchisers in a specified area—much like a manufacturer's representative. The franchise agent acts for the franchiser in recruiting franchisees for operating outlets. Ordinarily, you must offer considerable managerial and selling experience before franchisers will consider appointing you as their agent.

Operating Branch Franchise

Although sometimes thought of as an operating franchise, the branch franchise does not truly qualify as a franchise. The "franchiser" owns the outlet, supplies the know-how, and hires a manager. Many of these managers work under a "franchise agreement" that ties their earnings and profits to operating results, but they operate more as employees than owner-operators. The growth of branch franchises recently, results mainly from a shortage of capable, management-oriented, motivated men and women with enough capital to buy and operate their own franchise. Some of the major, big-ticket franchises, such as *Holiday Inn,* have bought out many of their original franchisees because they prefer to operate them as branches for a variety of reasons. The original franchisee usually turns a neat capital-gains profit in the process.

HOW YOU CAN FIND YOUR
FORTUNE-BUILDING FRANCHISE

Big franchisers, like *International Industries, City Investing,* and *Kentucky Fried Chicken,* operate and show increasing profits each year because they are well managed and provide franchisees with proven packages of products and know-how. But, like most fast-growing, lucrative industries, franchising has attracted a group of "fast-buck" artists who operate on the fringes of franchising. These "fly-by-nighters" operate mainly in the "front-money game." That is, they sell fancy promises along with a package of equipment and/or a big inventory of parts or supplies. They profit almost entirely from the initial sale. After you buy the equipment or inventory, they couldn't care less whether you succeed or fail. Their glowing pitch about continuing management service turns out to be empty promises or a sketchy booklet.

When investigating or choosing a franchise, rely on the people who know for advice—your local Better Business Bureau, the National Better Business Bureau, your local Chamber of Commerce, and your friendly banker. Also, you can systematically investigate a franchiser's claims on your own by—

Checking Out the Franchiser

Find out for yourself the answers to the list of questions that follows. Don't depend entirely on the franchiser's sales representative or accept all the facts in his sales brochures—find out for yourself. Your banker can look up the company in his Dun & Bradstreet guide. If the franchiser is listed on the New York Stock Exchange or the American Stock Exchange, you can find data sheets in Standard & Poor's reports at your local library. The Business and Defense Services Administration of the U.S. Department of Commerce publishes a yearly listing of franchise companies with data on each franchiser, such as number of franchised units, capital requirements, type of operation, training available, longevity in business, etc. A recent issue of this guide, *Franchise Company Data for Equal Opportunity in Business,* carried data on 284 franchisers operating in the United States. Questions you should ask include—

● When was the business established and how long has it been offering franchises? How many franchised operators are currently in business?

● What kind of reputation does the franchiser have among the operators currently holding franchises? Ask the franchiser for a list of nearby outlets. Take a trip to visit one or more franchisees. You should spend a full day with at least one operating franchisee of the company you are considering. Check the franchisee's experience with the franchiser—

—Does he consider the franchiser fair?

—Does the franchiser actually provide the promised services?

—Which of the restrictive clauses—if any—in the franchise contract chafe the operator?

—Is the franchise developing the profits expected?

—In addition to questioning the operator, observe the business. How many customers come in?

—What do the customers buy and how big is the average check or bill?

—Are the customers satisfied with the product or service? If your investigation and questioning of one franchise operator turns up a solid negative reaction—bad-mouthing by the operator, less than expected business volume, or differences in expected purchases—don't reject the franchise without at least a cursory investigation of a second operation. You may have picked the bad apple in the basket. The point is—investigate thoroughly yourself—*before* you sign any agreement.

● Will the franchiser reveal openly certified figures indicating net profits of more than one operating franchisee? Don't depend on "typical" balance sheet presentations or "expected operating profit statements." Ask particularly for the data on a nearby franchisee, so you can check out the figures yourself. You may find that this data is considered "confidential." But, you should insist on seeing some reliable indication of actual, rather than projected, operations.

● What kind of training will the franchiser provide? Is training included in the franchise fee? Or, do you pay your own expenses separately? Some franchise agreements call for transportation allowances, living expenses, and cash payments as part of the training package included within the overall franchise fee. Training provisions vary widely among franchisers; just make sure you understand exactly what you will get—then evaluate whether you believe the training is adequate. For example, ask an operating franchisee whether his training was just barely adequate or more than adequate to get him started.

● What kinds of assistance will the franchiser provide—and for how long?

—What kind of market research will the franchiser supply to help you locate customers?

—Will he help you find a location and design the remodeling of an existing building or a new building?

—Will the franchiser help you train employees?

—How about financing? Will the franchiser invest some of his own money in your franchise as a loan or will he assist you in borrowing capital from a bank or other source?

—What kind of promotion will the franchiser provide? Does the franchiser advertise nationally? Locally?

—What kind of merchandizing help can you expect—sales aids, point-of-sale assistance, advertising copy?

—How does the franchiser provide this continuing support—through a supervisor who calls regularly or only when you request help?

● What is the financial strength of the franchiser? Does he have the funds to carry out his expansion plans—and to help you with your financing?

● How have previous operators fared? Have any of them failed? How often do operating franchises change hands?

● What do you expect the franchiser to do for you that you cannot do for yourself? Establish a list and evaluate the advantages and disadvantages of a franchise compared to opening a similar business on your own.

● Compare the offered services of competing franchisers if you have an opportunity. Most popular franchise operations have attracted more than one franchiser. One may exhibit a better track record than the others. Unless you investigate more than one franchise chain yourself, you'll never know which offers you the best opportunity.

• How is the franchiser organized? Is the parent company essentially a one-man operation or are there specialized staffs available for you to call on for advice?

Evaluating Your Interests

Picking a franchise is much like getting married—you look over a number of interesting possibilities before finding just the right girl—or franchise. But, once you pick one, you're married to one—and must ordinarily steer clear of all the other interesting possibilities that were formerly available. So, check out your own assets and interests by asking yourself the following questions as a minimum—

• Do you like the kind of business you will be engaged in when you begin operating the franchise outlet? Have you actually flipped hamburgers and sold food to the public if you're considering one of the many fast-food franchises? Do your interests and abilities lend themselves to the specific franchise you are considering? Are you ready to commit much or all of your remaining business life to a specific franchiser?

• How much capital will you need to buy and get the franchise operating profitably—and do you have it? Most of the capital requirements listed by franchisers amount to absolute minimums. You should have ready access to more than the required minimum or reach a clear understanding with the franchiser about how much capital you really have. Unless you will be starting your franchise operation on a moonlighting basis, consider if your capital is sufficient to cover living expenses until your operation reaches the break-even point.

• Are you prepared to sacrifice some of your independence of action in exchange for the advantageous program of the franchiser? Are you prepared to accept the rules, methods, and procedures laid down by the franchiser even if you may not agree with all of them?

Evaluating the Franchise Agreement

You need the help of your own lawyer in studying the

franchise contract clause by clause. In fact, many of the big, reliable franchisers will not sign a contract until you have consulted your own lawyer. Some of the questions you or your lawyer should ask include—

● What kind of protection from other franchise operators does the agreement provide? Will your franchise award you an exclusive territory? Is the franchiser connected with another company that offers competing franchises? If so, how are you protected from encroachment on your territory from these franchisees?

● Does your franchise agreement limit you to one outlet—or can you open more than one outlet within your exclusive territory? Will you receive similar start-up and continuing assistance to establish second or third outlets?

● Under what conditions can you terminate the franchise agreement? What options does the franchiser reserve for termination? Can you sell your franchise and take a profit for the goodwill developed? Must you sell out to the franchiser, or can you sell to an acceptable new party? Termination provisions can be particularly important if you find your interests are not compatible with the franchise business.

● What binding agreements are included in the franchise contract for purchase of supplies and equipment from the franchiser? How about exclusive services—accounting, group purchasing, insurance protection, advertising, etc.? If the agreement calls for these services, how are the prices determined and are they competitive with similar services available in the open market?

● What will your costs be under the franchise agreement? You should know, exactly, the amount of the initial fee—and what it includes. What extra charges, if any, may be tacked on? How are continuing charges, percentages of sales, or royalties figured?

● Does the agreement specify the products you will sell, operating conditions, and conformance requirements? Can the franchiser force you to sell new products in the line when introduced?

● What provisions does the agreement provide for arbitration of differences between you and the franchiser if such differences should develop? Does the agreement require you to maintain a specific sales volume under threat of revoking the franchise?

Franchise contract agreements are unique—no two of them

read alike. The agreement provides an illuminating clue to the intentions and reliability of the franchiser—use it wisely, and study it intently, at least overnight. The sharp operator, for example, will sometimes not make a copy of the agreement available for you and your lawyer to study. Remain alert—just because a proposition carries the magic title "franchise" doesn't mean that it is an automatic route to riches and wealth. The "fast-buck" artists spiel out the riches available, they play the "American Dream" theme—where most of us would prefer to be independent businessmen, and they fool a good many prospects every year—enough to set off Congressional hearings into franchising practices. Your protection—hardheaded, thorough, personal investigation of the facts. And, when you collect the facts, don't examine them through rose-colored glasses. Analyze the facts for what they tell you—not what you would like to see. Remember, once you sign on that dotted line— you're committed for a long time.

9

Selling--Your Key
to Big-Time Earnings

When you learn to sell effectively, you're in the big-money leagues for life. Every business and industry depends on sales. So you write your own ticket when you produce orders. Sales offers the chance to start by moonlighting. But, don't expect to step lightly into a high-paying sales business of your own without training and a breaking-in period of learning. To start your own sales-oriented business—

- *Examine the potential possibilities of establishing yourself as a manufacturer's representative, particularly if your background is technically oriented.*
- *Take over a territory as an independent, commission salesman.*
- *Start with part-time selling.*
- *Look into after-50 opportunities.*
- *Invest in training to assure success.*

"Nothing happens until somebody sells something," a quote from Arthur H. Motley, publisher of *Parade* magazine, highlights why salesmen earn high pay. Sales are the key to profits—so anyone who can really "move the goods" earns a healthy slice of the income produced. Check these points—

- Sales incomes increased more during a recent three-year period than any other group's income. Figures compiled by the Research Institute of America, Inc. show salesmen's pay climbed 18 per cent, executive compensation 17 per cent, middle-management and professionals (doctors, lawyers, and dentists) 14 per cent, and clerical and production workers 12 per cent. During the same period, the cost of living as measured by the Consumers Price Index rose 8.6 per cent.
- Presidents of 27 per cent of America's corporations scrambled to their pinnacle through sales and marketing, according to a survey by the Council on Opportunities in Selling, Inc.
- During the first year following a switch from some other occupation, salesmen finishing a professional sales training course averaged a 34 per cent increase in income—with some incomes up as much as 300 per cent.
- Salesmen ranked second in the list of average incomes—entertainers captured the top spot at $25,000 plus per year. Salesmen were next at $20,000-$22,000, followed closely by the medical and law professionals at $18,000-$20,000. When these figures were compiled, only 2 per cent of the working population earned $19,000 per year or more.
- Producing salesmen frequently earn more than the president. In one Ohio manufacturing company, two salesmen earn more than the president—however, he's glad to pay them because their sales keep the company alive and prospering.

Examples of men and women who doubled or tripled their incomes by switching into sales come more easily than for any other profession. Take the case of Don Elmers, former Director of Music Education in a fashionable suburban junior and high school system. Don inspired students to plug away at their band instruments, beginning in the fifth grade. He and his associate director turned out one prize-winning group after another. But,

Don was caught in a salary schedule fixed by his graduate degree and years of experience. He couldn't earn another nickel despite how good he might be as a teacher. At age 30, the road ahead looked bleak with only a minimum increase in salary programmed, a schedule that always seemed to lag behind yearly increases in the cost of living.

To break out of the trap, Don registered in the Sales Training, Inc. (STI) program called "Whole Man Development." For six months he studied on his own in the evening while continuing to work days at the school. After spring classes closed, he attended STI full time to graduate as an honor student. Immediately he went into insurance sales. The high school lost a talented and inspiring music teacher—but Penn-Mutual Insurance gained a highly motivated, professionally trained salesman. Within three months, Don was selling at the rate of $1,200,000 of insurance per year plus occasional special-purpose coverages he arranged as a broker to meet unusual requirements. One month out of three he topped applications and sales for the local office. His estimated increase in income—about 150 per cent. How did he do it? Several factors are important—

> ● Don radiates enthusiasm. He transferred the same kind of infectious spirit that motivated kids to practice their horns into sales presentations for a product he believed in—whole life insurance.
> ● He works hard, scheduling meetings with prospects as early as 7 in the morning for breakfast to as late as 8:30 in the evening. During the middle of the day, he processes the never ending piles of paper. Does he mind the long hours? Not at all—because he is excited about his job—and his excitement shows and pays off.
> ● Professional training in sales techniques, confidence, and motivation building, plus a continually increasing knowledge of the immensely complex insurance business contribute to Don's sales ability.

Is Don happy about changing from his first love of music and teaching to selling insurance? "Of course I liked teaching music. That's why I spent so many years in college. But, now I have to pinch myself every morning just to make sure I'm not dreaming. Changing to sales was the greatest thing that ever happened to me."

CHANGING TO SALES

Change appears to be the order of the day for many successful transplants from dead-end jobs, income-limited jobs, military careers, and from one kind of selling to another. Just a few examples—

● Harry K—trained himself intensively for law enforcement work and worked for the Denver county sheriff's office, but, in time, he found that looking at the wrong end of a gun could be disquieting and not financially rewarding. So, he began servicing dictation equipment, utilizing his Army electronic training in radio, radar, and electronics. The job of servicing equipment also promised limited long-term potential. So Harry, never one to give up easily, started once again, this time in sales. While continuing to work at service and repair, Harry enrolled in Sales Training. He earned the first vacancy in the dictation firm's sales staff. Immediately his volume of sales took off. He knew the equipment from the inside out. During the first full year after completing his training, sales volume expanded and his income tripled over his earnings as a service representative.

● Stephen W—found himself with a severance paycheck and no job shortly after passing his 50th birthday, a casualty of a merger. Although he had spent 25 years with his company, the shakeout of middle and near-top management personnel when the new top brass took over found him in that all-too-familiar position—too old to find a new job in planning and budgeting and too young to retire. Discouraged after more than three months of looking for another management position, he decided to make a fresh start. "Nobody in personnel can tell you outright that you're too old for a job they have in mind," Stephen reported. "That would be illegal, discrimination due to age. But, you get the message after being turned down again and again." With his usual analytic approach, Stephen examined every likely possibility. He didn't have years to build up a new reputation. He was a man in a hurry to begin earning his $25,000-plus salary again. At the end of every road he looked at, the same sign loomed—SALES. He made another wise choice and sought out a complete, professional training program for sales. By attending classes full time, he finished a complete sales training course in half the normal time. Job opportunities immediately opened. He started selling office supplies full time. In less than one year his net earnings topped the $25,000 annual rate he had spent 25 years attaining—with no ceiling in sight.

● William R—faced another kind of problem. He retired from the Army with the rank of Major after 22 years of service but with no professional or vocational training. His boys were in junior high school. College expenses loomed over the near horizon. Retirement pay without the allowances he had learned to live with wouldn't meet his desired standard of living. So, Bill took his disciplined mind into sales. His mature approach and military bearing helped him to sell mutual fund shares for a local brokerage firm. But, too many prospects failed to buy, and he was about to lose out when an associate suggested he learn more about the psychology and mechanics of selling. Training followed, and even before he was through with his training his volume doubled—and he is still completing sales at an ever increasing clip.

With so many opportunities—really good opportunities for increasing income—available, why are so many lucrative sales jobs going begging? Probably the answer lies in the image conjured up in people's minds when they hear "salesman" or "selling." Try it yourself—what pops into your mind first when you hear the term salesman? Do you think of the door-to-door type who knocks at your front door with a case of pots and pans? Or the "student working his way through college"? The high-pressure used-car pusher and fast closer who confuses more than helps? Possibly the sales agent for a here-today-gone-tomorrow home improvement contractor with his "special deal"?

Dramatists have done little to brighten the image of selling as a profession. *Death of a Salesman* with its highly dramatic message and caricature of the back-slapping, man-to-man salesman probably set back the profession of selling more than any one example of negative image building—despite the play's dramatic success. Harold Hill in the *Music Man* similarly characterized the "drummer" image associated with selling. Despite the picture of selling instilled in many minds, a salesman's status and how people feel about his job may affect your decision to change. The image and the salesman's performance and self-satisfaction are improving. For example :

Recently, the President of the United States said: "The salesman is a key figure in an economy which relies upon individual initiative and the competitive forces of the marketplace to stimulate full employment and achieve an orderly and efficient distribution of our goods and services. Our salesmen and saleswomen are the creative organizers of the free market so vital to the growth, prosperity, and well-being of our nation."

Answers from a survey of nearly 1,000 of the biggest corporations in the U.S., as reported in *The Salesman— Ambassador of Progress,* a publication of the Sales and Marketing Executives-International, clearly note the increasing status of salesmen—

- "Salesmen are becoming more important in our business"— 79 per cent.
- "We are employing more salesmen than we did five years ago"–74 per cent.
- "Business profits do not come from making things—profits come from *selling* the things that business makes"–92 per cent.
- "No, we do not think salesmen suffer from a low social status"–92 per cent.
- "Absolutely not!" 92 per cent of the chief executives replied in answer to the question—"Do you think that salesmen have questionable ethics?"
- "Would you, as sales managers, counsel your sons to go into selling?" Answer–96 per cent—"Yes!"
- Wives answered—"My husband travels a lot, of course, but our lives are more exciting. I have traveled with him and, when possible, our boys go along. We've seen more of the country than most families. I've seen his profession (selling) grow in stature and his income triple over what we thought possible. The great big difference is that my husband doesn't have to work a 'schedule.' I've

found that a salesman who does well sets his own schedule in life; his own income level; and, yes, even decides where and how he wants to live. He's not so restricted by the controls or 'yardsticks' of other professions. I'm glad I married a professional salesman."

Good salesmen enjoy greater security than men in most other professions. When business conditions fall off generally, good managers keep their salesmen because they are the ones who bring in what business might be available under depressed conditions. No company can exist without sales and the salesman is the man who brings in the sales. During the great depression of the 1930's, more salesmen were fully employed 12 months a year than men in any other kind of work.

What does it take to make it big in sales? One maxim, again from *The Salesman–Ambassador of Progress,* accepted by all successful salesmen, is: "Selling is the best paid hard work— and the worst paid easy work." Salesmen working on commission are, in effect, in business for themselves. They are paid only when they produce. Even if they draw a small salary or are paid a draw against commissions, they don't last long unless they produce. Few jobs or professions face such a direct challenge—such a direct relationship between income and effort. Hours are seldom fixed and frequently extend beyond eight hours a day. Selling is hard work—definitely not the life for anyone who isn't willing to "put out." The hours and the work pace account for much of the turnover in selling jobs. For example, statistics over more than 30 years indicate that only half of those who start to sell insurance are still selling at the end of one year. After three years, only 20 per cent are still at it.

While some salesmen are born—most salesmen, even those with the gift of persuasion, can benefit from objective training. Selling combines many skills into one profession—psychology, sensitivity to human problems, absorption in human relations, interpersonal communication—plus specific knowledge of the product being sold. Modern, successful selling adopts the by-words—"Selling is serving."

SALES OPPORTUNITIES THAT PAY OFF BIG

Computer Hardware

Shemwater-Boldt, who started as two partners, quit their unimaginative electronic engineering jobs in a big company. The two sensed opportunities for marrying a variety of specialty electronic equipment to the big computers being sold by IBM, Honeywell, and others. Tape-to-card converters, remote inputting, specialty printers, and character analyzers were just a few pieces of the exotic hardware that were coming off the lines of small, high-technology companies. In the remote Pacific Northwest, these companies could sell only by sending one of the officers on occasional trips. There was no service available nearby. So, Dale Shemwater, an electronics engineer, contacted these small, upcoming companies and offered his services as a Technical Sales Representative—more generally known by the title of manufacturers' representative. The response was so great, he and Steve Boldt joined forces to form their own sales firm. Now the firm hires four full-time technical salesmen plus two full-time service men and the inevitable office help.

Shemwater-Boldt operate by studying company requirements and matching these requirements with the machinery they have for sale. They engineer the requirement at times by pointing out to a computing department the savings in time and money possible if they used one or more of their machines. Cost savings provide the opening wedge. Unless one of their machines will cut a company's costs, there's little likelihood of a sale. Shemwater-Boldt act as systems analysts. They study a whole system, looking for applications where the equipment they know and understand can increase a company's efficiency. There are no glad-handing, big entertainment bills for buyers, and few really personal relationships. A sale depends on showing a dollars-and-cents improvement in operations, and savings must be dramatic to pay for the investment usually in only two or three years.

Note the elements that fit together into a successful pattern for Shemwater-Boldt—

● High-technology field—Both Dale and Steve graduated in electronics engineering and spent years in design and field service. They understood their own machines—and how they interface with customers' machines. Much of their time is spent working out the bugs that inevitably crop up when their machines are married with a customer's computer. These debugging sessions involve sleeve-rolled-up digging and all-night involvement at times. But, they know their business, their machines, and how to tackle problems.

● Stand-alone business—Shemwater-Boldt own their business and contract their sales know-how with specific companies in exchange for an exclusive territory. The companies they represent pay Shemwater-Boldt nothing unless they sell. But, the commission on sales runs as high as 25 per cent of the sales price. High—but still less costly for a small company than maintaining its own branch sales office or attempting to sell so far from their home office.

● Selling, the key—The partners must sell in both directions. First, they sell their services as technical representatives to producing companies and negotiate contracts fair to both. Second, they sell the products of the companies they represent, often in competition with other representatives selling similar equipment.

● Changeable business—Success in selling one company's products may go too far, and Shemwater-Boldt may be dumped by the company. When volume builds to a point, a company may decide to establish its own branch office. With enough volume, branch office expenses may cost less than the commission being paid to Shemwater-Boldt. Or, a company may delete a product from its line—customers for specific units may be limited because of a product's special nature, or a competitor may offer a better product at less money. So, the partners continue to evaluate new products and look into new fields for expansion. Recently, Shemwater-Boldt took on a complete line of specialized numerical-control computers for controlling automated machine tools.

Salesmen look at problems as opportunities, and Shemwater-Boldt continues to expand. The pay is good—Dale Shemwater lives in a waterfront home, moors a huge cabin cruiser at his own dock, and his family drives three cars. Dale's income ranges toward $100,000 annually.

In-House Salesmen

Selling pays off inside big companies, too. Not only do sales-oriented executives move up rapidly into executive suites, but they earn high salaries as they advance. When Phil H—took over as sales and service manager for a hydraulic equipment firm, the job involved more service than sales. So, Phil moved into sales for a specialty steel manufacturer. Within one year, by concentrating his efforts strictly on sales, he increased the declining steel division's sales volume by 300 per cent. His plans to double sales again within three years project a need for added production capacity. Credit for the increase in sales and profits goes directly to Phil—and he was rewarded with a salary increase that doubled his pay earned as the sales and service manager for the hydraulic firm.

Territory Selling

Operating with a sample case and order book, the modern territory salesman closely resembles old-time "drummers" but with a difference—keen competition and sophisticated buyers. Tom F—represents a high quality cutlery manufacturer. Although on the payroll, Tom operates independently and draws commissions only. He pays his own expenses, both for travel and entertainment, and his commission rate allows for such expenses. Such an arrangement forces management decisions on Tom, as he must decide when traveling will pay off and when it won't. Decisions to entertain buyers fall into the same category. Tom operates truly as an independent businessman, making decisions daily on whom to contact for business, how to outfox the competition, the selling approach to each department store buyer, and, of course, how many calls to make and where to concentrate his efforts to meet factory quotas. Many selling opportunities call for similar management decisions.

Tom applies many of the skills he has learned from

training sessions and hard-knock experience. Interpersonal communication and an understanding of human nature affect his performance because, as Tom will tell you, "There's very little difference in quality between our knives and our competitions' knives." When product differentiation is slight, personal selling ability, honed to a fine edge by training, really pays off.

PART-TIME SELLING—YOUR KEY TO BIG-TIME MOONLIGHTING PROFITS

Look around—opportunities for you to expand your income through part-time selling exist everywhere.

But, you should be aware of the pitfalls. Part-time selling washes out close to 90 per cent of those who start for two main reasons—

- Opportunities in part-time selling call for skilled, motivated salesmen.
- Goods and services available for part-time selling frequently call for door-to-door selling, one of the most difficult selling environments. Good salesmen with persistence earn fabulous per hour incomes selling pots and pans or encyclopedias door-to-door. One Business Administration student averaged $17,000 every year for four years while he attended the University.

Despite the inherent problems, the following examples typify the earning capacity of selling part time—

- *Correspondence Courses*—Mail-order schools advertise widely for students for nearly every trade and vocation. Personal follow-ups and sales from inquiries lead to exceptional earnings. There are no "cold calls." A west coast school of drafting, for example, sells a complete, well-designed, and developed course priced at $600. For every course a salesman sells, he earns $85 commission. Selling occurs mainly after dinner because potential students are looking for a way to educate and advance themselves. So, the moonlighting salesman spends two or three hours several nights a week following up on inquiries mailed to him by the home office. Once he signs up a client, the home office handles all training and collections on time-payment plans. All the salesman does is sell the course and he nets an average of $200 each week. Similar opportunities are available for all the large correspondence schools.

● *Mutual Funds*–Salesmen willing to work during the evening hours and on weekends find selling mutual funds part time profitable and satisfying. First, sales are mainly to professional people and others with cash to invest. Second, calls are follow-ups to inquiries. Third, fund selling usually requires a license and customers respect the salesman as a professional. Commissions are relatively standard at 2 to 4 per cent of gross sales which usually run into thousands of dollars.

● *Real Estate*–Weekends and weekday afternoons are key selling times for residential property. So, housewives and moonlighters can sell houses and land while working at their regular jobs. Most states require would-be real estate salesmen to pass an examination to earn a license. Commissions on houses or lots don't happen often, but–wow–when they do, they pay off around 2 per cent of the selling price for houses and about 3 per cent for lots and land.

● *Party Plans*–Dresses, underclothes, shoes, kitchenware, and household supplies are only a few of the products sold by getting a group together after dinner for a showing. People like parties, and some kitchenware sales plans offer a complete dinner for guests. Party plan selling is particularly effective with *Tupperware,* an outstanding example. Pathway Products also expanded sales when they switched money-makers, with earnings averaging $10 to $50 per hour of invested time.

SELLING—THE AFTER-50 OPPORTUNITY

Like the merger-displaced executive, men and women over 50 face reduced opportunities. Between the ages of 45 and 50, many men recognize they are not going to make it into the president's chair–time is running out on them. They feel trapped in middle-management or dead-end slots. Yet, many are not ready for retirement just yet. Women may be free from the everyday chores of raising children at close to the same age. Selling offers an "out" for both men and women if they are motivated and willing to work. Maturity and experience become advantages in selling real estate, travel, investments, insurance, technical services, and products—the full line. Resistance to change prevents many unhappy men from going into sales. Yet, there is no future for "obsolete people" trapped in dead-end jobs.

YOUR STEP-BY-STEP GUIDE TO BIG-PROFIT SELLING

Determine first whether your personality can be tuned to selling. You do this through testing. Contact your local state employment service (the address will be in the yellow pages of your telephone directory) and ask for counseling assistance. Some people will never make good salesmen. You may find that the counselor can arrange for testing as part of the state services. Or, the counselor will offer you a selection from unbiased testing services for which you will pay. Don't depend on a selling ability test administered by one of the sales training schools. Some of these schools use the test as a device for attracting students and few applicants "fail."

If your test indicates an aptitude and interest in selling, get the best training you can afford *before* tackling your first selling job. You wouldn't attempt to design part of an airplane without engineering training or prescribe medical care without attending medical school. So, don't assume you can sell without training.

Schools offering training in sales, selling methods, practical psychology, and motivation for selling operate principally in two sections: during the day to train industrial and business sales personnel for in-house positions and during evening hours to train ambitious men and women who sense the opportunities and want to get into selling. You'll find a variety of opportunities for sales training in your community. Check these—

● Junior college and high school adult education programs offer courses in direct selling, public speaking, psychology of selling, and specialized courses in real estate and investments to help you pass state exams for a sales license. If you live near a major college, investigate their day and evening class schedules for courses related to sales training.

- Join one of the Toastmaster clubs to gain experience in speaking and confidence in expressing yourself.
- Investigate one of the privately operated schools specializing in training for sales. One major school is *Sales Training, Inc.* (STI) with head offices in Seattle, Washington. STI began teaching salesmanship only 13 years ago. Now it operates 17 branches in the United States and Canada. Nationally, STI graduates 2,000 trained salesmen from their "Whole-Man Program" every year. The school addresses much of its course work to positive attitude and confidence building, motivational training, and mental conditioning. Role playing in simulated selling situations affords experience, and these sessions are taped for playback on TV so that students can see their own mistakes and correct them.

Success Motivation Institute operates nationally through franchises. SMI's approach is aimed at building confidence and motivation to carry through in sales and other activities.

Dale Carnegie Schools offer sales training as one of their options in addition to executive training.

Look for these and other schools in the yellow pages. Your local state employment counselor may suggest another avenue for special training rather than a full program.

- Read from the hundreds of books published on just about every element of selling. Check your local library. Behavioral research and applications have laid new foundations for understanding and teaching salesmanship. *New Psychology of Persuasion and Motivation in Selling** by Whitney, Rubin, and Murphy, 1965, *The New Handbook of Sales Training** by the National Society of Sales Training Executives, 1967, and *Selling–A Behavioral Approach*** by Joseph Thompson are typical of the new order that emphasizes motivation, human relations, interpersonal communication, and role playing in learning how to sell.

Select your selling opportunity only after carefully analyzing several from leads in your newspaper classified section, state employment service, private employment agency, or individual referral. Check into these aspects and evaluate them carefully—

---

*Published by Prentice-Hall, Inc., Englewood Cliffs, N.J.
**McGraw-Hill, Inc., New York, N.Y.

• Will you be given additional on-the-job training? Insurance companies, mutual-fund houses, and part-time sales organizations often provide specialized training and aids for selling their own product or service.

• Will you be comfortable selling the product or service? Can you tell your friends about your selling activities with pride? If you can't, you should look for a different opportunity.

• Will you be required to buy inventory or pay a franchise fee? Any opportunity that requires a substantial cash investment should be checked with the Better Business Bureau, your banker, and operators in other areas—references furnished by the franchiser.

• What are the earning possibilities? Check these just as carefully as you would your own business opportunity. Develop high and low projections, then check your answers with actual earnings from salesmen in the same line of selling.

Preparation through training, selection from opportunities through detailed evaluation, and sticking to your plan will improve the odds of your success in selling a thousandfold.

10

How to Raise Money
for Your Own Business

Money to make money—that's the role capital plays in your business. Money or an equivalent, such as "sweat equity," can come from many sources. Sometimes, to avoid under-capitalization, you tap them all. You learn how to—

- *Figure how much money you need.*
- *Develop a plan to acquire the money you need.*
- *Use SEM (Somebody Else's Money) to finance part of your business.*
- *Call on the Small Business Administration for help.*
- *Discover little-known sources for venture capital.*
- *Apply substitutes to reduce capital needs.*
- *Play the "little bit from many" game to borrow funds.*

Money—yours or somebody else's—means survival and profits. Study after study points out these salient facts—

- Lack of money, undercapitalization, or whatever you call it leads to about one-third of the business failures recorded.
- Money available for operations and growth promote profitability—"them that has do better than them who don't" or "the rich get richer."

Both of these points demand your attention. You can't escape the need for money to start, maintain, and expand your business.

YOUR FORTUNE-BUILDING PROSPECTS WITH SEM (SOMEBODY ELSE'S MONEY)

"Borrowing money to make money" makes sound business sense. Here's why—borrowing money (by whatever method you choose, as defined later) enables you, as the profit-oriented owner of a business, to expand sales, introduce new products, and decrease costs. Any one or all of these effects in combination should increase earnings more than the cost of the borrowed funds. For example, suppose you borrow $10,000 at 8 per cent interest. At the end of the year, you will pay the banker $800 for the use of the funds plus the $10,000 principal (just to keep the figures simple). However, the $10,000 for a year enables you to build parts worth $40,000 when sold at retail at a cost of $20,000. A factor of two to one is not uncommon in make-or-buy situations for a small company. So, by borrowing $10,000 you rent equipment and hire labor, and save $20,000 on the cost of parts you sell or install as part of your business. At the end of the year, you pay off the loan plus the interest and retain a profit of $9,200.

Take an even more common example. You are pressed for funds in operating a retail or service business. So, you use suppliers' credit as part of your capital. This simply means that you order things from a wholesaler on credit. You hope to turn over the goods and collect cash from your customers in time to pay the suppliers' bills by the 10th of the following month. Your suppliers' funds become part of your capital. Most suppliers recognize that extending credit increases their cost of doing business. Money is a capital resource just as much as a delivery truck. Everybody pays rent for using money; the rent is called interest. But, instead of raising their prices to everybody, suppliers frequently offer a discount for prompt payment. Invoices may read—"2 per cent 10, net 30." Such notation offers you a discount of 2 per cent of the total billing if you pay within ten days. But, if you don't have the cash, you wait the full 30 days and pay the full amount. You are, in effect, paying 2 per cent for using the money (credit extended) 20 days. On an annual basis, 2 per cent for 20 days amounts to 36 per cent interest on equivalent capital. To take advantage of cash discounts, you need a revolving cash fund big enough to carry purchases with your own money. By borrowing an amount equal to your purchases for 20 days at 10 per cent, you earn the difference—or 26 per cent. You can look at this transaction either of two ways: first, by using Somebody Else's Money (SEM), your business earns a 26 per cent return on purchases completely outside your buy-and-sell activities; second, by reducing your costs of capital, you can price your goods and services competitively with other properly financed businesses.

When Mike Kinder took over the failing drive-in (see Chapter 4) and turned it into a $30,000 profit in one year, he invested practically no money of his own. Note these steps—

- Mike agreed to take over all obligations of the owner-manager, simply by agreeing to pay off the $45,000 bank loan outstanding. The owner gave up his equity to protect himself from further losses. The bank permitted Kinder to assume the loan because of his proven credit and known managerial ability.
- Supplies for the first month were delivered—again on Kinder's credit.
- Wages and promotional expense were his only out-of-pocket payments.
- At the end of one year, the drive-in business had become so

profitable that Kinder sold his equity (difference between outstanding debts and capitalized earning capacity) for $30,000. But instead of taking the appreciated value in cash (probably impossible, since the chef didn't have it), he accepted a note for regular payments and interest at 8 per cent. Kinder invested no long-term capital of his own in the venture—only his established credit. The bank and certain suppliers provided the required capital—Somebody Else's Money (SEM).

GETTING THE MONEY YOU NEED TO START YOUR BUSINESS

You will need money in your business at least twice: (1) when you start, and (2) when you need to expand your business. Requirements for getting money differ at these two stages. So we consider getting money to start first. Later, we consider raising money to expand and enlarge your business.

Find How Much Money You Need

Too little capital may mean failure before you ever get started for any one of a variety of reasons. Statistics muddy the primary cause for failures, and many failures termed as "managerial incompetence" may really have been financial failures. Aside from the specter of outright failure, too little opening capital adds these problems to your others at start-up—

- Limits your stock of goods for sale.
- Reduces your ability to advertise and limits your other business-development activities.
- Forces you to use credit at noncompetitive rates.
- Penalizes pricing due to an excess of fixed costs (loan interest, lease payments, etc.) during start-up phase.

All of these problems point up the need for a firm plan—particularly a financial plan—before you start. Chart 10-A defines a bare minimum Financial Plan. Note that it consists of two parts, start-up expenses and operating expenses.

CASH REQUIREMENTS	RENT	BUY
Start-Up Expenses:		
1. Facilities Down Payment		
2. Equipment		
3. Inventory		
4. Legal		
5. Advertising & Promotion		
6. Miscellaneous —		
a. Licenses		
b. Telephone Installation		
Sub-Total		
Operating Expenses — Per Month		
1. Rent		
2. Equipment rentals		
3. Interest (if any)		
4. Wages		
5. Taxes		
6. Utilities		
7. Miscellaneous		
Sub-Total		
Total		

CASH AVAILABILITY	SOURCE	AMOUNT

Chart 10-A. *Financial Plan.*

Start-Up Expenses

These will occur only once. Later you may incur one-time expansion expenses. But, let's consider each of the one-time costs for starting your business—

- Facilities include your base of operations (shop, store, or factory), exclusive of equipment, tools, or inventory. If you can operate out of your home, the cash required to get into a shop or facility can be zero. If you are starting a restaurant, you will probably have to pay an initial fee when you sign a lease, even if you pay only the first and last months' rent. Any changes made to a facility before you can open fall into this category too. Take the restaurant again as an example. Space rental includes no funds for installing equipment for decoration, a sign out front, or built-ins. Whether you call stoves, sinks, counters, and booths equipment or facilities can be arbitrary. One useful determiner—if it is portable and can be carried away, it's equipment. Money for anything built-in, such as a lighted ceiling, plumbing for a dishwasher, and the like, is part of the initial facility. Depending on your type of business, initial facilities investment can be substantial. Some of this investment must be paid for in cash—plumbers, carpenter labor for rearranging cabinets, partitions, etc. To pay for other parts you invest "sweat equity" by painting the place yourself, installing new floor tile—even installing your own cabinets, partitions, counters, etc. Here you must consider the rent paid during the added time it actually requires you to get the facility ready for operation.
- Equipment—Ovens in a restaurant, tables and chairs, dishes —all of these items are used and reused rather than expended. You can either buy them or rent them. Consider both alternatives in your Financial Plan. Two factors govern your decision to rent or buy—

    —Cost of rental vs. buying. You figure your rental cost penalty (and rental will usually cost more than buying outright) by totaling the annual cost for monthly rentals. Compare this cost to the interest you would pay if you bought the equipment. For example, suppose a used oven for a restaurant cost $1,000. Or, you can rent the oven for $120 per month. Over the year, rental payments total $1,440. Compare the annual rental ($1,440) to the cost of borrowing the $1,000 at 12 per cent interest. Your cost—$120 for the year, assuming no payment on the loan principal. The difference between $440 and $120 or $320 represents the penalty you pay for renting vs. buying.

　　—Cash available. Despite many obvious advantages of buying your equipment, you will probably not have enough cash to buy what you need. So, you rent—and the penalty becomes another of those costs of undercapitalization. Renting vs. buying also reduces start-up risks. But, you need to know the difference in costs between renting and buying so that you can assess relative penalties. Compute totals on both bases—rent and buy—and enter these amounts on your Financial Plan.

　　● Inventory—Some businesses, such as a retail clothing store, depend heavily on stocking enough variety and sizes of each item to serve customers. Too little inventory turns customers away—and they don't come back. An excessive inventory, on the other hand, strains your start-up finances and depresses profits as a Return on Investment (ROI). The kind of business you start, your competition, your experience, and how much money you can raise all affect the level of your inventory.

　　●Legal, advertising and promotion, and other miscellaneous items will vary widely according to your kind of business and whether you start small or go all-out at the beginning. But they all cost money, and possibly there are others you should know about that are not listed in Chart 10-A.

Operating Expenses

These are recurring items that continue as your business continues. The most obvious ones are noted in Chart 10-B(p.185). Again, consider each item in turn—

　　● Cost of goods sold may be small in a service business, such as TV repairing, or a sizeable portion of sales, as in a restaurant or a retail store. In a drive-in restaurant, for example, cost of goods sold covers all of the food supplies, plus the paper cups, napkins, and disposable items used in the serving of food, and direct labor. In a TV repair service, only the parts replaced are included and the major cost accrues as wages (yours or a helper's). Costs of goods sold vary directly with the volume of sales.

● Rent and equipment-leasing fees are payable monthly and change very little relative to volume.

● Interest on invested capital, loans, etc. must be considered as an operating expense. Such interest payments are directly chargeable against income in computing taxes.

● Wages can be considered partially variable and partially fixed relative to business volume. One crew size can handle a minimum or maximum number of customers. You can change the number of employees for each limit—but not much in between. Wages include fringe benefits and your contribution to Social Security collections, plus any state assessments for a variety of services.

● Taxes include sales taxes, income taxes, and the myriad of other items, from a Business and Occupation levy to annual licenses and permits.

● Utilities include water, gas for heating, rubbish removal, electricity, telephone, and sewer.

● Miscellaneous expenses include everything not specified in the others, such as insurance, legal fees, accounting services, repairs, etc.

Your operating expenses are likely to vary considerably between your first, sixth, and twelfth months. Therefore, don't consider only the expenses for one month's operations in your Cash Requirements. Instead, develop your Operating Plan for a full year. Chart 10-B defines the same elements noted in your operating expense plan, but extends them for the full year. You need to estimate, as best you can, operating revenues you can expect beyond the start-up period. For example, if your Operating Plan estimates a loss for the first three months, you must provide for that amount of cash—or equivalent—in your start-up Financial Plan. Under any circumstances, you should estimate the capital required for at least the first month's operations. You may substitute unpaid family labor as free. Unless you allocate a reasonable cost to this investment of labor by you, your spouse, or older children, you cannot calculate your real cost of doing business or true profitability. Consider unpaid family labor at no cost only to reduce cash requirements during the initial start-up.

		Monthly											Annual	
	1	2	3	4	5	6	7	8	9	10	11	12	Total	%
SALES														
COST OF GOODS SOLD														
Purchased Goods														
Labor														
Sub-Total														
OVERHEAD														
Rent														
Sales Expense														
Interest														
Repairs														
Equipment Depreciation														
Taxes														
Sub-Total														
PROFITS (LOSSES)														
RETURN ON INVESTMENT														
PER CENT OF SALES														

Chart 10-B. *Operating Plan.*

Accumulating the Capital Needed

Cash Requirements, one part of your Financial Plan, defines how much cash you need. Now, where can you find the cash? Following are the usual sources—

● Personal resources—Savings still form the first choice for funds to start a new business. Teamwork, with a wife working to save money to start a business instead of improving the family's standard of living (for the short run), accumulates funds faster than prying dollars out of a single paycheck. A moonlight job helps to build up savings quickly. Personal savings are important in any financing plan because bankers look at your investment in detail—unless you are fully committed, a banker will not ordinarily consider investing his bank's funds. In addition to personal savings, consider refinancing your home mortgage, selling some of your assets (expensive car, boat, trailer, a vacation home, rental house, etc.), borrowing on your insurance policy, or selling stocks acquired in the past (a form of personal savings).

● Loans from outside sources—Banks remain the first choice for short-term capital—three months to a year. Whether you decide to borrow from a bank or not, talk with a loan officer anyway. You get an outsider's scrutiny of your plan without paying a consultant's fee. A banker will insist on details—your Financial Plan in developed, written form for a starter. You will be amazed at the kinds of information a banker will insist on knowing before he puts money into your business—so be prepared. The discipline of applying for and backing up your requests for a loan can pay off handsomely—even if it turns out that your best bet is not to start your business. Hard-nosed advice at the beginning could head off many impending business failures—possibly yours. Banks supply the following kinds of funds—

—Commercial loans for specific periods—usually 30, 60, 90, or 120 days. Use these funds for short-term variations in volume; for example, to finance the purchase of an extra stock of toys for the Christmas season. Interest costs are simple to figure and vary according to risk, size of loan, condition of the money market, and your use of the funds.

—Installment loans—usually for longer periods than commercial loans, possibly for up to five years. Installment loans work much like a loan you take out to buy a car. Interest and a part of the principal are paid back each month. At the end of the period, you will have paid back the loan and all interest due in regular installments. Commercial loans, in comparison, are paid in full at the end of each period. Interest may be discounted (paid at the beginning) or added on at the end.

—Term loans may extend even longer than installment loans. If you can get a term loan, it becomes part of your long-term capital. Banks will require collateral—and some will insist on a regular review of your operations—possibly even a director on your board if your company is a corporation.

—Special-purpose loans—to finance accounts receivable, warehouse receipts for stock, equipment leases, etc.

—Line of credit denotes a bank's willingness to loan your business money as needed up to a defined limit. You borrow and pay interest on the money as you need it without a new application each time. Usually, a line of credit is limited to well-established businesses rather than a new entry.

—Participation loans combine a loan of money with some other kind of financing—a loan from the Small Business Administration, equity investment by a Small Business Investment Company (SBIC), a nonprofit foundation, or a business-aiding group. Participation loans usually result from special situations—and always from detailed and special planning.

●Loans from special sources—Specialized financial services provide funds for specific purposes, such as—

—Factors who advance money against accounts receivable. A factor may buy your accounts receivable at a discount. The factor collects from your customers, assumes the credit risk, and charges you a fee for his services. Depending on your type business, and your need for capital, your credit and collection management abilities, and the condition of business, factoring can aid your business. Generally, factoring increases the cost of money compared to a straight bank loan—but you get additional services.

—Small Business Administration loans if participation loans (see above) or a guaranteed loan are not available. The SBA loans money directly only when money is not available elsewhere and your credit meets SBA requirements. The SBA loans money for as long as five years at reasonable rates against various types of collateral—land, buildings or equipment, warehouse receipts, chattels, or personal endorsements. Your best bet, if you believe you might qualify for a SBA loan, is to visit one of the SBA field offices.

● Sell stock or equity in your company or proprietorship. Check with your state securities department if you intend to sell shares only within one state. The Securities and Exchange Commission gets involved if you intend a wide distribution of stock. However, you can sell limited amounts of stock to a few investors without registering the stock. Sale of an interest in an unincorporated business falls outside the jurisdiction of these security watchdog agencies. However, if your business is technically oriented, it offers considerable profit potential. Since you need several hundred thousand dollars of long-term equity capital, you might consider a public stock offering. If you do, get competent help from an experienced underwriter. The details of such a stock offering are beyond the scope of this book.

More practical is the sale of stock to one of the SBIC's. These Small Business Investment Companies are regulated and licensed by the Small Business Administration and sometimes borrow money from the SBA. Ordinarily, the SBIC sells its own stock to raise funds for investing in new, high-risk companies. SBIC's can invest in a corporation for a stock (equity) interest. They also loan money to individual proprietorships. Sometimes they do both—buy stock and loan money—to a corporation. Most SBIC's prefer investing in a new company in exchange for stock which they hope will grow in value and provide capital gains rather than simple interest on loans. When an SBIC takes an equity position, it also takes an active role in the company management—particularly financial management. Access to such professional assistance may be worth more to you and your business than the loan or investment—so, don't overlook these possibilities. Contact your banker or Chamber of Commerce for leads to SBIC's in your community.

Local and state development funds specialize in financing

small, starting businesses. The Southeastern Pennsylvania Development Fund, one of the sponsors of the Regional Development Laboratory in Philadelphia (see Chapter 5) operates specifically to aid new companies or firms with loans and financial counsel. Your state's Department of Commerce or your local Chamber of Commerce can help you contact a new business development fund in your community.

● Limited partnerships enable you to raise money from many investors much like the sale of stock. For many uses, mainly in real estate transactions, limited partnerships offer tax-shelter benefits for investors that are not available to stock purchasers. If you operate in the real estate field, check the possibilities of organizing a syndicate of general and limited partners to acquire and/or operate property. Leverage and depreciation affect earnings, so that partners receive more spendable tax-free income than from many stock investments. States regulate the formation and operation of limited partnerships closely to protect public investors. Since these state regulations vary widely, look into the specifics for your state if your business involves real estate. Limited partnerships can be a large and valuable source of funds when conditions are "right."

HOW TO SCRATCH UP THE MONEY YOU NEED

Your Financial Plan highlights the gap between the money you need and the funds you can raise (your own plus what you can borrow). Even if you scrape up the bare minimum, you should have access to more money—just in case. Franchises, for example, note the minimum amount of capital required—with emphasis on MINIMUM. Whether for your own business or a franchise, you'll probably need more money than you think—experience proves it. If you're typical, you will underestimate money requirements; either because from your inexperience you estimate low or forget, or in your enthusiasm and excitement to get started you skip lightly over money problems. One word of caution at this point—DON'T underestimate money needs. Face up to your capital requirements squarely—*before* you spend your capital resources—not AFTER, when you desperately need more money to continue. When an honest gap between cash available and cash required exists, try the following ideas.

Collect Your Sweat Equity

Time and effort can sometimes substitute for cash. For example, Arnie Carriloni (see Chapter 1) bought a used pizza baking oven for 20 per cent as much as the cost of a new one. He completely rebuilt the oven in his spare time while he planned ahead. Even while rebuilding the oven, he was not committed to opening his pizza place. He could have sold the rebuilt oven at a profit. But, by investing a small amount of cash, plus a bundle of time and engineering know-how, he reduced his cash requirements. Other ideas you may use to develop sweat equity are—

> ● Scrounge low-cost materials for remodeling a shop, store, or other facility. Note the sources for cut-rate paint, building materials, used plumbing, etc. in Chapter 4.
>
> ● Barter your expertise, time, and effort for something you need. Harriet B—traded several of her best pots for photographs from a professional. Then, she used the photos to develop promotional literature that helped her sell to stores. Her craft products became trading material—better than money when dealing with a creative photographer. A large space in a booming shopping center was to be cut up into three stores. So, Oscar H—, a part-time carpenter, made a deal. He built the partitions, installed a new ceiling, new doors, and other changes necessary to make each of the business spaces self-sufficient. In exchange, Oscar obtained the lease for one of the spaces rent-free for a year—and the developer saved more than contractor estimates.

Buy Used Tools and Equipment

One of the most underrated resources in our country is the used market for practically everything—from salvaged building materials, to furniture, to hardware. When Frank Sweeney decided to lease a service station, he needed tools—so he watched the classified ads and shopped the used equipment market. By picking and choosing, he accumulated a full chest of wrenches plus specialized tools—and a full range of auto diagnostic and tune-up equipment for about 25 per cent of the cost if he had purchased them all new. Practically anything is available used. Sometimes you need to refurbish it before use—a good application of sweat equity. Don and Janis P—took on a whole roomful of badly used restaurant booths and tables. The pieces were replaced during renovation of a restaurant. Together Don and Janis recovered each of the cushioned booth seats; Don stripped off the old plastic laminate and glued on new tops for the tables. When they finished, they had equipment worth $4,000 new for only $600 in materials plus just under 250 hours between them.

Tap New Sources for Funds

Play the little-bit game—raise some of the money you need by borrowing in $10 or $25 amounts. You'll find borrowing $25 from ten friends, relatives, or associates easier than borrowing $250 from one friend. You might also sell future goods or services at a discount—$25 gift or merchandise certificates at a 20 per cent discount. In addition to raising money from your friends and relatives by loans or sales of goods or services, consider these possible sources—

● Credit union—If you plan to continue working at your regular job and start your new business moonlighting, borrow from your company credit union—or one of the other credit unions you may have access to.

● Lodge, union, or pension funds—Local administration of these funds often makes them available to friends—but only as prudent investments. You can expect the same hard-nosed scrutiny from a fund manager as from a bank loan officer.

● Private investors—Your banker, or some other friend within the big business clique, might put you next to an individual with funds available for special situations—like your new business. Robertson Aircraft, for example, modified a special airplane in exchange for working capital during its early stages. Individuals may insist on a "piece of the business" as well as interest on their money. But, these individuals will put up risk capital when the opportunities appear ripe for a major gain. Just watch your step and don't give up an excessive interest in your business for a few bucks.

MONEY TO EXPAND YOUR BUSINESS

Once you get your business under way—sales progressing satisfactorily, income increasing, most of your borrowed capital paid back, and profits over and above your salary coming in regularly—what next? You'd like to expand your business. Growth doesn't just happen. Successful businesses plan for growth—building and selling new products, opening a new store, expanding the line of products sold. Chart 10-C depicts a general-purpose look five years ahead with a rising sales volume projected. Note that the uppermost sales volume is not defined. What new product or service must you develop to keep the sales volume expanding? As older products and services decline, they must be continually replaced with new ones. You face two problems in long-range planning—

- Where will the added sales come from?
- Where will the funds needed to expand the sales come from?

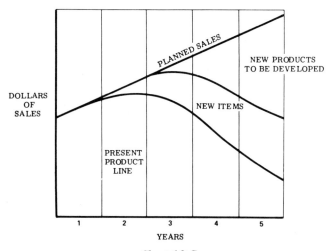

Chart 10-C

For example, Robertson Aircraft's long-range plan calls for continued development of new STOL-mod kits for other airplanes (see Chapter 5). Unless new items for existing models and new airplane kits are developed, sales can be expected to fall off with time. So, product development figures big in any long-range planning.

Planning works effectively even if you are a service-station operator. Examine your options—stay open longer hours; add a second or third lift to increase grease, oil change, and the repair capacity; expand tire business aggressively; or advertise and promote greater sales with coupons, games, or other means. Your business grows because you plan for growth—then put your plan into action.

Planning your capital requirements follows the general scheme shown in Chart 10-D. Note the five-year look ahead. Begin with Gross Sales for each product line as a reference. Follow through with the major elements necessary to achieve your planned growth of sales—

- Product development calls for expenditures ahead of sales to try new ideas, test their market acceptance, develop manufacturing or selling techniques—everything necessary to develop new or improved business opportunities to expand sales volume.
- Facilities are those long-range expenses necessary to produce new products or more of the old line—factory space, sales branches, laboratory facilities, etc.
- Personnel needs go up with increased sales. So, you must plan for recruiting and training new people.
- Accounts receivable grow as business volume expands—sometimes at an increased rate compared to present volume.
- Inventory of parts in work or in finished stores increase with growth in sales—so money must be available to finance higher inventory volume.
- Sales promotion—advertising, exhibits, personal sales forces—all are needed to reach projected sales growth, and they all require additional money.
- Other costs will depend on your kind of business—management training, transportation costs, etc.

YEAR AHEAD

ITEM	1	2	3	4	5
GROSS SALES					
PRODUCT A					
PRODUCT B					
PRODUCT C					
OTHERS					
TOTAL					
CAPITAL REQ'D					
PROD. DEV.					
FACILITIES					
PERSONNEL					
ACCTS. REC.					
INVENTORY					
SALES PROM.					
OTHER					
——					
——					
SUB-TOTAL					
CAPITAL AVAIL.					
DEPRECIATION					
RET. EARNINGS					
SUB-TOTAL					
INVEST. REQ'D					
LOANS					
EQUITY					
OTHER					

Chart 10-D. *Five-Year Plan.*

Your job in long-range planning is to project growth in sales along with the capital and labor required to achieve that growth. Part of the cash for growth investment can come from depreciation allowances and retained earnings. When you determine how much additional capital you need each year, you can arrange to acquire the funds through a variety of means—

● Loans may be desirable to retain your share of control and stock (if your company is a corporation). With a profitable operating record, loans for expansion are relatively easy to obtain at reasonable rates.

● Equity financing through a sale of stock to the public may be a way to achieve two goals: (1) raise the money you need for expansion, and (2) sell a portion of your interest in the company for a major capital gain that puts more spendable cash in your own pocket.

● Other means—a merger with another company, a sale of bonds to an insurance company, or a sale-leaseback of certain facilities owned in part or in full by your company.

Acquiring the funds you need for expansion will be easier than raising funds to start your business—particularly if you develop a detailed, five-year look ahead along the lines of Chart 10-D.

11

Special Situations--How to Convert Them to Profits

Fortunes pop up from unexpected places for those alert enough to recognize an opportunity and run with it. Most special situations happen only once—like that opportunity knock—so be prepared. Here's how others have seized the unusual quirk and turned it into their own private fortune. Use the following as idea starters; then come up with your own. Some examples—

- *The abandoned-trademark or free-patent trick.*
- *Gold and precious metal treasure you may find.*
- *Real estate and its profit potentials for the innovative developer.*
- *Doing the technically "impossible" with old airplanes.*
- *A new way of selling used cars directly.*
- *Minting real coins as well as collector's items.*
- *Government research activities, your free source of profit-making ideas.*

Opportunities for turning a specialized skill, a once-in-a-lifetime situation, or a natural idea whose time has come into a private fortune lie around like gold nuggets just under the surface. Your job—uncover them. Few people recognize an idea's potential until an imaginative innovator pulls off a major deal. Then, observers may pooh-pooh the whole affair. Meanwhile, the innovator is packing off bills to the bank.

THE ABANDONED TRADEMARK TRICK—FOR TREATS

Remember *Ipana* toothpaste? During the 1930's and 1940's Bristol-Myers ballyhooed the name from big-time radio shows—"Ipana for the smile of health." In 1946 *Ipana* sales totaled about $17 million and accounted for 20 per cent of the toothpaste market. But, the decay-fighting, "Look, Ma, no cavities" toothpastes with fluorides knocked *Ipana* out of the big-time market. Production stopped and the trademark was abandoned. Later, two enterprising Minnesotans picked up the *Ipana* trade name for free, contracted with a chemical manufacturer to start making toothpaste, and began marketing *Ipana* toothpaste again.

Apparently, memories are strong. People remembered *Ipana* toothpaste. With no advertising, the two promoters, Elliott Royce and John Howe, sold $250,000 worth of the new *Ipana* in the first seven months. Not bad for a business that the two started with only $3,000. The two work only about ten hours a week and a secretary comes in three days a week. The new formula for *Ipana* includes stannous fluoride—just to be competitive. Even more competitive is a typical price at retail of 57 cents compared to the nationally advertised brands at 77 cents for the same size tube. The two partners are planning to extend the name to other products, such as a mouthwash.

Remember *Moxie?* Even earlier than *Ipana*, *Moxie* was a drink that battled the big names for sales. With its euphonious ring, *Moxie* lasted longer than the drink as a slang term for "energy and courage"—a dictionary definition. More meaningful is a definition that aligns *Moxie* with "swinger." First brought back to life by *Mad* magazine, the idea of resurrecting *Moxie* as a drink hit James C. Wickersham and Frank A. Armstrong. The two picked up the ball and began pushing *Moxie* with a new, modernized flavor. Regional tests proved successful, and *Moxie* expanded nationally.

Revival of the 1914 Stutz *Bearcat* and the 1923 Stutz also traded on a long-standing memory. The new cars are produced in small quantities in Tulsa, Oklahoma—a long way from Detroit—by the Stutz Bearcat Automobile Co. The new *Bearcat* claims a unique spot in today's car offerings—plainly aimed at "the man who has more money than anything else."

Central to each of these revivals is a sense of what the public will buy—plus nostalgia. Each was a "special situation"— one you couldn't create but one that was there.

Special situations depend on promotion through publicity. *Ipana's* new promoters spend nary a nickel on advertising. News stories, sparked mainly by the mouth-dropping bravado of the two enterprisers at bringing back an old, familiar trademark from the dead, spread the word widely and quickly—including a major feature in the *Wall Street Journal* and a brief mention in *Time. Mad* magazine pushed *Moxie* back into the public's vocabulary. And, the car and mechanical magazines splashed the *Bearcat* on their editorial pages.

A list of currently registered trademarks is maintained as a public record at the Patent Office, Washington, D. C. Trademarks expire 20 years after registration and are considered abandoned unless renewed. However, common law rights may still reside with the original trademark owner. To assure clear title, negotiate with the owner for permission to register his trademark. If this is not feasible, consult an attorney who specializes in trademarks and patents for advice on registering an abandoned trademark for your own use.

TREASURE IS WHERE YOU FIND IT

Looking for treasure—metal coins and jewelry, lost bullion boxes, and pots of gold—now occupy serious hunters equipped with an electronic gadget that looks like a big pan lid at the end of a long stick. The Goldak Co. of California makes one of several available treasure finders—more properly termed a metal detector. You use it by moving it over an area with the pan lid just above and parallel to the surface. Surprising caches of coins and jewelry are found under the surface of beach sand, particularly after a busy summer. The treasure finder sniffs out metal objects like the mine detectors used by the military. When the detector passes over a hidden metal object, the sensitive electronics set off a whistle. You dig around the area to unearth the metal. It may be a coin or a bottle cap.

Serious treasure hunters use similar detectors to locate hidden caches of coins in old buildings, particularly in old mining areas or deserted cabins. Wet sand or earth improves the searching, as moisture makes ground more conductive. Right after a big storm is the best time to search a beach area, with prospects of picking up thousands of dollars in coins, jewelry, and shipwreck items.

Want to try prospecting? Instead of laboriously panning for gold the way old-time prospectors did, try *The Little Prospector,* a gold-finding machine invented, patented, and produced by Leo and Harry Smith of Kennydale, Washington. *The Little Prospector* weighs 16 pounds, is powered by a 3/4-horsepower gasoline engine, and floats at the end of an anchored tether on aluminum floats. The machine separates out the dense material from sand and dirt with centrifugal action. The Smith brothers—one a prospector in Alaska and other areas for years, the other an engineer and confirmed "tinkerer"—say that a professional can separate and recover about 85 per cent of the gold that passes through his pan. Amateurs recover even less. *The Little Prospector* enables the amateur to recover 90 per cent or more of the gold. To operate the gold-finding, mechanical prospector, the treasure seeker shovels sand and dirt into the machine as it floats. *The Little Prospector* throws out the dirt and concentrates the gold-bearing sand into a small box. A dedicated shoveler can process as much as 10 tons of material a day. In a creek or river where a professional panner can show $5 for a day's panning, *The Little Prospector* can show $50, a ten-times advantage. In the West there are thousands of miles of gold-bearing creeks and rivers ready to be staked—and with the blessing of the U.S. Bureau of Mines. The United States needs all the gold it can find and produce, so amateur prospectors are encouraged to look while on camping vacations and weekend trips into wild areas. But, the Smith Brothers are making their gold from *The Little Prospector* with orders backlogged and production behind schedule.

Diving for sunken treasure calls to mind sunken galleons long buried in Caribbean waters. But the four Pearce brothers of Port Angeles search out a different kind of sunken treasure—timber logs that have sunk to the bottom of the cold waters in the Strait of Juan de Fuca. Literally, billions of board feet of timber rest under water around Puget Sound and the Strait. About 2 per cent of the logs in storage booms soak up too much water and sink to the bottom. Although many of these sinkers cannot be salvaged, the ones that are accessible are free to the finder. The Pearce brothers "mine their sunken treasure" by searching out sunken logs. A diver attaches tongs or a "choker cable" to one of the submerged logs. A crane on a floating platform lifts the sinker to the surface. Empty oil drums attached to the slimy logs keep them from sinking again. One by one, the string of raised logs grows longer as the day peters out. At the end of the day, the buoyed logs are towed to a sawmill. There, the mill processes the waterlogged sinkers to keep them from sinking again.

Hazards are plentiful in Pearces' work—total darkness at times in the water, slick and slimy logs that make movement among them treacherous, huge octopi that have occasionally wrapped one of the brothers in a giant tentacle, and sharp-toothed lingcod that grow up to 6 feet long. Killer whales sometimes surface in the waters they are logging. At those times, the brothers stay aboard the float. Weather interferes with their underwater logging too. Rain and snow don't bother them—but when wind builds swells on the water that reach 10 feet from crest to trough, they leave. A change from conventional diving equipment to scuba gear doubled their production because the self-contained equipment enabled them to move around underwater more freely. But, the scuba gear created one big problem—getting lost under the floating log booms that may extend for acres to shut off light. Despite the hazards, constant watchfulness and care pay off, and the underwater forest of logs grows larger each year.

Trash forms another lucrative hunting ground for treasure, with silver, gold, and platinum plentiful in industrial scrap. So plentiful is treasure in the trash barrel that Handy & Harmon (850 Third Ave., New York, N.Y. 10022) published *A Book About Trash* that tells how to locate, segregate, handle, and ship precious metals found in the trash heap. The book is written strictly for the novice and tells how to institute a precious-metal recovery program. You can do what many others have done because "treasure is where you find it."

FIND THE "DO-THINGS" IN REAL ESTATE
FOR CREATIVE PROFITS

Oscar Rowley turned his profit-sensitive eye toward a need for inexpensive housing in his Texas town. Two needs were evident to his practical eye—housing for student couples with little cash and couples with small children where the husband was stationed at a nearby Air Force base. Both needs for housing called for rentals—not sales. So, Oscar located several big old houses in the city. Some were being lived in; others were vacant—too big for a single family. Oscar picked up the houses for very little more than the land cost and with a mortgage based on land alone. In one house, he invested less than $1,000 of his own money—he borrowed the rest (SEM).

His next step was to remodel the houses into small one- and two-room apartments and housekeeping rooms. New doors and entrances provided access. More of a problem was kitchen equipment. A one-piece sink, oven, cooking surface, and cabinet was installed in each set of rooms. Where possible, he added a bath; at other locations, he expanded the existing bathroom for multiple use. By controlling costs, he added six apartment units in one building for a cost of less than $5,000 overall. Rentals averaged $60 to $90 per month depending on size. Collections totaled $480 per month.

Note that with $1,000 invested in the property and $5,000 in facilities improvements, he pulled in more than $5,000 a year, allowing for vacancies. In less than two years he had recovered his investment. Further, depreciation on the full value of the property (including mortgaged value) sheltered his income from taxes. With the sheltered cash flow from his first building, Oscar repeated the process with a second building— and then a third and a fourth. By scheduling acquisitions and renovations according to cash flow, he invested no further money in the business after the initial $6,000. Yet he became a major landholder in the area.

What about zoning and building permits? Most of the houses were located near or within areas zoned for apartments or commercial development. To relieve the crush on housing, local officials granted temporary building permits to cover the renovation. Several years later, the rentals crush over, the temporary permits were revoked on certain of his buildings in nonconforming zones. By that time, the value of the land had risen—so, he sold out—taking a neat capital gain profit on the depreciated value of the property. At the end of ten years, Oscar had recouped his original $6,000 and taken an additional $120,000 out of his holdings, with several properties still to be sold. And remember, real estate management was a part-time activity for Oscar.

Can you duplicate this special situation? Its very possible —note the combination of events that contributed to Oscar's fortune-building success—

- A shortage of low-cost housing that was likely to continue for years—college students and Air Force personnel. Both groups moved in and out of the area regularly to create a transient demand.
- Availability of big houses that could be converted to apartments for a minimum of capital investment. The resulting living quarters cost one-half to two-thirds as much as new construction. Oscar bought houses built on large lots. So, the land valuation provided a floor under the price paid for land and house.
- Zoning or availability of temporary permits allowed Oscar to remodel without violating local ordinances. Sometimes houses are remodeled into small apartments illegally, but such activities are risky at best—and mostly unnecessary.
- Low remodeling costs—most important of all, Oscar spent as little as possible in remodeling. Rather than spend several hundred dollars running plumbing lines to a couple of rooms, he equipped them only with a simple sink and cooking top, combined with a refrigerator, and rented the space as "housekeeping rooms." Toilet and bath facilities were down the hall. Close cost control enabled him to offer rentals at the lowest possible cost.
- Rent collection jibed with paychecks. Oscar made it a point to be around when students or military personnel arrived with their paycheck to collect rent.
- When the land became more valuable than the income from rental, Oscar worried little about esthetics or the history of the old houses. He demolished the house when the land was worth more without the house than with it.

You can follow Oscar Rowley's part-time route to a fortune in real estate by sniffing out your own opportunities. Sometimes "reverse synergism" prevails. Instead of a whole being worth more than the sum of its parts (synergism), the parts by themselves may be worth more than the package. One-time special situations in real estate fit the reverse synergism tag. For example—

Along Lake Michigan's shore area, north of Chicago, many delightful old houses were built in the early 1900's when servants were available and a man's status depended on the number of rooms in his house and the land surrounding it. But, since World War II, big houses on expensive land became a drag on the market—many were taxed beyond support. So, Neal B—investigated. He found big, stone houses sitting on lake-front sites with as many as 10 acres of land. The house may have been modernized, but it was huge. Few families could afford or wanted such a big house. So, prices were way down—and still nobody wanted them. So, many stood idle.

Neal took a different tack. He looked beyond the obvious. He figured the potential value of the land without the house. Attempts to cut up the big old houses into small apartments were rejected—with vigor. Big old houses were in zones limited strictly to single-family residences. Each case was different, but he found a pattern—buy the house and land, salvage parts from the house, but tear it down, divide the land into single-family lots, and sell the developed land to builders. It worked. In just one case, he took over the mortgage on a 40-room mansion sitting near the lake front on a 12-acre lot—all enclosed within a high masonry wall. Total price was $180,000—covered entirely by the mortgage he assumed. With an eye for value, Neal supervised salvage of the house—carved bannisters on the stairs, beautiful paneling, huge plate-glass mirrors—even the cut stone from the exterior walls were preserved and sold at auction (a new trick in itself). With the house site leveled but with the masonry wall remaining, Neal laid out 32 new homesites with winding lanes entering and exiting through masonry gateposts in the wall—some old and some new. Depending on location relative to the lake and their size, the new building lots were priced from $12,000 to $22,500 each. Neal's cost and income picture looked like this—Original purchase, $180,000 (none of the money his own). Lot development cost $43,000. His take—$1,500 profit on the house (value of salvage sold less teardown costs) and $512,000 gross on lot sales. Net profit after all costs—$289,000 or a return of a little over $6.70 for every dollar of his own invested (exclusive of the mortgage money which was somebody else's).

What did Neal B—do to deserve such a whopping payoff? First, he envisioned a completely different picture than others saw in looking at the big old house on valuable land. Second, he didn't let nostalgia or a romantic feeling for the "good old days" stop him from tearing down the delightful old house. Third, he used publicity generated by some critics to publicize the auction sale of materials salvaged from the house—for his profit. Also, he retained some of the old charm by retaining the masonry wall around the "estate." The wall served two purposes—protection and an "insider" feeling for lot buyers. Fourth, he designed the lots to meet minimum zoning standards. Finally, he priced the lots above normal values to assure building of quality homes, even though his holdout tactics extended selling time.

Can you duplicate either of these special real estate situations? Opportunities abound. You need imagination, a thorough knowledge of zoning and real estate values, vision as to what can happen in the future to land values in your specific area, and a willingness to risk your capital for a multiple gain. You can reduce your risks by: (1) working in the real estate business—selling houses part-time, even looking at open houses on Sunday afternoons as a means of getting inside professional information; (2) keeping your eyes and ears open to trends in employment and economic news that could impact your area; (3) using SEM whenever possible. But, don't figure on doubling or tripling your money in one year without some risk—the earnings go along with the risks. Sometimes you might lose.

OLD-TIME AIRPLANES PROVE TO BE FORTUNE BUILDERS

How do you transport something that's too wide for train tunnels and highways? By boat? Too slow when the product is destined for space flights. So, John M. Conroy and Les Mansdorf joined forces to build the "Guppies"—oversize airplanes based on Boeing's original *Stratocruiser*. Conroy was the pilot who conceived the idea and Mansdorf owned a fleet of retired Model 377 *Stratocruisers.* Conroy designed a huge, oversized body structure to be built onto a 377 chassis. The size of the new body disregarded every aerodynamic rule known—a new model tested in a wind tunnel won grudging approval that it would fly—but nobody was absolutely sure. So, the partners built the "Pregnant Guppy" with 29,187 cubic feet of internal cargo space. The National Aeronautics and Space Administration (NASA) immediately contracted to haul oversize Saturn 5, Gemini, Agena, Apollo, Centaur, Pegasus, Surveyor, and Titan assemblies from California and St. Louis factories to New Orleans and Cape Kennedy.

The first Guppy flew in 1962. Since then, Aero Spacelines has built a "Super Guppy" with 49,790 cubic feet of cargo space, a "Mini-Guppy," smaller than either of the others, and is continuing to build more. On new versions, turboprop power plants replace the less powerful piston engines. Even with turbine power, the 25-foot diameter, whale-shaped body of the Super Guppy reduces flight speed by 80 miles per hour. Enough of the Guppies are now available to contract commercially for hauling outsize cargo. Major wing sections for Lockheed's L-1011 commercial airliner will be hauled across the country by the expanding Aero Spacelines.

Aero Spacelines represents an uncommon special situation—converting a used and practically worthless airframe into an aerodynamicist's nightmare and making a major success of it. John Conroy simply wouldn't be "turned off." Some people said his Pregnant Guppy wouldn't fly, but it did. Imagination, confidence in your own ideas, and the willingness to go ahead when you know you're right are "musts" to profit from your special situation.

USED-CAR AUCTIONS—A REVERSE TWIST

Regional used-car auctions, commonly referred to as the "dog shows," normally sell used cars only to dealers. But, Stanley Gordon, from New York's Bronx, noted the millions of people who sell and buy used cars every year. He figured "Why not bring them together directly instead of through another dealer?" So, he opened his first Nation-Wide Auto Auction, Ltd. Even Stanley was surprised at how quickly the idea caught on. At only one location, Nation-Wide earned $35,272. The next year he opened other auction lots, and income spurted to $106,000 for the first three months and was heading up.

Gordon's success formula filled a need—bringing buyers and sellers together. His auctions work like this: You have a car to sell, so you drive it to Nation-Wide and pay a $50 fee. Nation-Wide will appraise your car and offer to buy it at the appraisal price. If you don't like the price, you put it up for auction. If the bid price exceeds Nation-Wide's appraisal value, you split the difference 50-50—otherwise, you are guaranteed the appraisal price as a minimum. Or, you can drive your car back home. In any case, you are out $50—most of which covers a complete checkup on a diagnostic machine like those in the big auto diagnostic centers. Buyers find the printed results from the diagnostic center checkup, along with an estimate of the cost to correct noted deficiencies, on each car to be auctioned. Even if you drive your car away unsold, you get a diagnosis of what is needed to fix it up.

How many used-car dealers and salesmen work at their trade in the U.S.? Thousands—yet one saw his "special situation" and converted what he knew best, selling used cars, into his own fortune-building business.

A FORTUNE DIRECT—MINTING COINS

Franklin Mint, the largest private mint in the world, stamps out 20 million coins every week in metals ranging from aluminum to platinum. Coin collectors have become so numerous that coins are scarce—so the Franklin Mint manufactures collectors' coins—and sells them by mail. During a recent year, the Franklin Mint sold more than $10 million for a $629,000 net income.

Franklin generates its own market by making up special sets—then creating a rarity market by limiting the number of sets coined. Stamping out coins or commemorative medals is no trick, but the design and engraving of the dies require skill and specialized machinery. Despite this cost, other private mints are beginning to stamp out coins to satisfy the lucrative collectors' market. Franklin Mint markets their coins and medals through imaginative promotions at a cost of more than $1 million of advertising and direct mail each year.

- Subscriber lists receive first chance at new commemorative medal and coin sets.
- A coin-a-month plan circulates among the mailing list, and production is limited to advance orders. A limit on sales builds a feeling of scarcity. The limited offer extends even to a waiting list. And unless by-mail collectors pay promptly, they are dropped from the limited-offer list.
- Special tokens for use in Nevada slot machines help to build volume for the stamping machines.
- Low-cost tokens as part of oil-company games also build huge volumes, but are produced sporadically.

Franklin Mint quality is so good, they make real coins for small countries with no mint of their own. Franklin's "special situation" started when the mint began developing commemorative medals after the supply of real silver dollars became far too small to satisfy demands. And, most of Franklin Mint's growth has been through mail-order selling.

SPECIAL-SITUATION EMPORIUM—YOUR GOVERNMENT

Pick a subject, any subject. Your government has probably more information on that subject than you can use—and it is all to your profit. The National Aeronautics and Space Administration (NASA) has piled up thousands of volumes of data and reports from which any number of special situations could be developed. Most of these research findings are free or open to license for a minimum fee.

Take just one subject—electronic medical testing and screening. The advances in technology developed to determine the physical reactions of astronauts (pulse rate, blood pressure, body temperature, etc.) in a simulator—or while walking on the moon—are being put to work in hospitals. Combining computers, X-ray and thermal photography, and medical electronics has cut the cost of routine medical tests in hospitals to one-quarter the former cost. And the surface has barely been touched. If you want to examine a few of the possibilities, address an inquiry to Scientific and Technical Information Division, National Aeronautics and Space Administration, Washington, D.C. 20546. Ask for their catalogs of Special Publications and Technology Utilization Publications. Or, order *A Survey of Space Applications* from the Superintendent of Documents, U.S. Government Printing Office, Washington, D.C. 20402, 70 cents.

Water as a crop? Would you believe $100 per acre each year? Water engineers studying how to conserve water supplies project that rain can be "harvested" from hilly areas by covering the hills with a plastic or rubberized fabric. Rain flows to the bottom of the hill and on to a reservoir. In the right places, a farmer could sell rain to a nearby city for more than crops might bring from poor soil. Note that 1 inch of rain over an acre produces about 25,000 gallons of water. Once the hills are covered, the more it rains, the more "crop" you have to sell. Rain-cropping hills is a study under way at the North Appalachian Experimental Watershed, a research facility of the U.S. Dept. of Agriculture. But, the Agricultural Research Service, the Department of Agriculture's research wing, has been revolutionizing farming since the 1800's. High-yield crops, for example, resulted from agricultural research. Data on wood and wood products pours out of the Wood Products Laboratory at Madison, Wisconsin. You can tap this lode of information by writing to the Agricultural Research Service, U.S. Dept. of Agriculture, Washington, D.C. 20250.

Another U.S. publication that can kick off ideas in a dozen directions is *A Survey of Federal Government Publications of Interest to Small Businesses.* For a detailed look at new reports that pour forth from government agencies, check copies of the *Monthly Catalog of United States Publications* at your local library. The range of research data from which you can develop your own "special situation" is truly staggering.

12

Where and How to Find
the Specialized Help You Need

When you decide to start your new business, you'll be asking questions. Those questions lead naturally to others—so, you need answers from a variety of sources. Check these sources of information—then find out everything you can before investing your cash, time, and energy.

- *Organization—which form is best for your business?*
- *Step-by-step route to incorporation of your business.*
- *Small Business Administration—how it can help you.*
- *SCORE counselors that provide detailed and specific consultation.*
- *How and where to ask for help from your state.*
- *Private and not-for-profit agencies you can ask for help.*
- *Taxes and your own private retirement program.*

Starting a business doesn't automatically make you smart in every field. All the skills, experience, and specialized know-how you need to round out your managerial abilities don't magically appear full blown. If you are a skilled serviceman, tradesman, artist, or engineer, you probably need business-oriented help to backstop your unique skills. You can't afford to neglect the vital business functions of organization, cost and tax accounting, planning, marketing, financial analysis, personnel management, and legal protection. And, the first of these is organization.

HOW TO DECIDE WHICH ORGANIZATION IS BEST FOR YOU

What are the differences? Basically, you only have three choices—

● *Proprietorship*—Here you simply own the business. You don't need government approval to begin operations. You can stop your business just as easily. So, proprietorships are inexpensive; any profits from the business are simply taxed as your own personal income, and you are personally liable for any debts incurred.

● *Partnership*—You and one or more others own the business. You need no government approval to begin operation, unless you designate general and limited partners. You begin a general partnership by signing an agreement among you and your partners, although an oral agreement can be just as binding. For tax purposes, the profits of a partnership are taxed directly to you and each of your partners. The partnership files only a tax information return and pays no tax directly on profits. Limited partnerships, however, require legal agreements conforming to state regulations. Limited partners, for example, enjoy protection from the unlimited liability of general partners. Limited partners can lose only the amount of actual cash or tangible property invested but cannot contribute services for value to the overall partnership. You must be aware of one notable hazard of general partnerships—unlimited liability. You or any one of the general partners can be held liable for all partnership debts without regard to original investment.

● *Corporation*—You form a legal "person" authorized by the

state to operate like an individual. Corporations exist only when chartered by a state, and the legal requirements and costs vary widely (see following section on steps for incorporating a business). Corporations may last forever, while proprietorships and partnerships are usually limited to the lifetimes of the owners or any one of the partners. Corporations may be limited in their business activities and profits are taxed directly and separately from the owners or executives (with one exception, the pseudo- or "subchapter-S" corporation).

Consider These Six Points Before Selecting the Form of Organization Best for You

Whether you ask the help and advice of a lawyer or not, you should analyze these factors—

● Costs and difficulty—All you need to start a proprietorship or partnership is a tax number from the state and possibly a license, depending on the business. If you operate under a name other than your own, you must usually register the firm name with the state. Partnerships are similarly easy and inexpensive to start, with the added desirability of some written or oral agreement among the partners—a written agreement prepared by a lawyer can protect you and your partners. Corporations cost the most, and you must file approved articles of incorporation with the state, pay fees on issued stock, and sometimes pay a start-up tax.

● Control of risks—If you elect to operate as a single proprietorship and incur sizeable debts, everything you own and your future income could be seized legally to pay off all your business debts. In a general partnership, you and every other partner incur responsibility for all debts owed by the partnership, regardless of the amount of your investment or that of any of your partners. Limited partners risk only the loss of their invested capital. At least one general partner is required in any limited partnership. Corporate structure limits your risk and that of any other investors to the amount invested. Creditors can force payment of their claims only to the limit of the company's assets.

● Continuity and longevity—A proprietorship exists only as long as the owner lives. The death or withdrawal of any one of the partners ends a partnership. Corporations, on the other hand, live a separate, continuous life of their own, irrespective of the withdrawal or death of any principal. Stock certificates representing ownership shares in a corporation may be transferred from one person to another, with or without permission of the corporation and without interfering with the corporation's operations.

● Administration flexibility and control—If you are the owner of a single proprietorship, you set the policy and operate the business as you see fit—for good or bad. As the "boss" you reap the profits or suffer the losses. In a partnership, depending on how an agreement may be worded, you must divide responsibility, control, and profits, if any, among you and your partners. Corporations, depending on size, may allow you to exercise effective control through a board of directors—or administration may be controlled by the shareholders of the business.

● Effects of laws on business organizations—Legal rights and obligations of single proprietorships and partnerships have been clearly established through the years. Mainly, proprietorships and partnerships must operate within the taxing and regulating bodies of laws. Our U.S. constitution guarantees to each citizen "all privileges and immunities," regardless of which state he may be doing business in. Corporate freedoms of action may be limited because each corporation exists under the articles of incorporation granted by a specific state. Out-of-state corporations can do business in another state but only by complying with special in-state obligations.

● Ability to attract capital—Financing affects all businesses at one time or another. The single proprietorship's principal fault is its limited ability to attract growth and operating capital in sizeable quantities. As a single proprietor, you are generally limited to your own funds or those you can borrow. Therefore, if you are planning a business that could require considerable capital, now or later, you should probably consider a corporation. Partnerships suffer some of the same limitations on capital acquisition as proprietorships, except that more individuals can contribute money and services. Limited partnerships enable many people to invest with limited risk. Sizeable amounts of capital are accumulated this way, primarily for buying real estate. Corporations can attract venture capital through the sale of stock. A corporation may also sell bonds either with or without a pledge of the company's assets as collateral. Direct loans may also be obtained from individuals, banks, the government, or other sources.

Corporations acquire capital in their own names, usually without reference to any specific individual.

**Advantages of a Partnership Compared to a
Corporate Organization**

In addition to the above points, note these advantages of organizing your business as a partnership rather than a corporation—

● Simplified taxation—Income, either as wages or profits, flows directly to the partners and is taxed as individual income. The partnership pays no taxes directly. Corporate income, however, is taxed at around 50 percent and only after-tax profits can be distributed to stockholders. The "subchapter-S" or pseudo-corporation can be one exception to this generalization. Taxes actually paid on partnership income vary according to your income.

● Losses, as well as income, are divided by partners according to the agreed shares. Also, the kinds of income, such as tax-exempt interest, long- or short-term capital gains, pass along to the benefit of each partner as if they were individuals. Corporations enjoy none of these privileges and are subject to special taxes (accumulated earnings tax or personal holding company tax).

● Partners, as real people, receive constitutional protection not available to the corporate "legal" person—example, the right against self-incrimination provided by the Bill of Rights.

● Partnership property may be transferred more easily among the partners than among the shareholders of a corporation.

● Simplified dealings with the state—Corporations must comply with batteries of legal forms and reports required by the state.

● Compensation of partners, either as reimbursement for expenses or the distribution of various kinds of income or profits, can be greatly simplified compared to distribution of corporate income. State regulations to protect minority stockholders also limit the flexibility of action of corporate officers.

Advantages of a Corporation Compared to a Partnership

On the other side of the coin are these advantages of a corporation relative to a partnership—

● Shareholders assume no liability for corporate debts while any general partner can be held for all liabilities of the partnership, regardless of his contribution.

● Only dividends paid are taxable to the shareholder, but partnership profits are taxable to the partners whether paid or not.

● Shares in a corporation can be used as collateral for a personal loan or assigned to heirs or someone else without corporate permission. Similar assignments of partnership interests must usually be approved by all partners.

● Compensation of corporate officers can be a flexible combination of salary plus stock options, deferred compensation, warrant options, and fringe benefits—tax-free life insurance, group medical and dental coverage, accident and health insurance, and invested savings plans. Partners enjoy few of these benefits.

● Corporations can borrow money more easily and from a much wider group of people or institutions than partnerships.

● Officers of a corporation are treated as employees; partners are not. The corporation pays social security taxes (company share), and expense accounts of officers can be fully tax deductible. Company facilities may be used with less comingling of interest by corporate officers than by partners.

● Corporations offer many more opportunities for estate planning because of the easily distinguishable shares of ownership compared to fractional partnership interests.

● Organizations can be planned and compartmentalized more easily in a corporation than in a partnership where major policy decisions usually require agreement among all partners.

Subchapter-S or Pseudo-Corporation

Some of the advantages of both the partnership and corporation can be acquired by electing to operate as a pseudo-corporation under subchapter S of the Internal Revenue Code. The pseudo-corporation enjoys all the features of a true corporation (it is actually incorporated under state regulations), but taxes are imposed only on shareholders—not on the corporation itself. As you would expect, a pseudo-corporation can exist only by complying strictly with a number of rules, mainly the following—

● No more than ten shareholders may own an interest in the subchapter-S corporation. Also, the ten shareholders must be individuals or estates—no corporate or partnership shareholders. Individual shareholders must live in the U.S.

● Only one class of stock may be outstanding for the corporation.

If all the formalities for subchapter-S election and operation are complied with, shareholders take profits with no tax imposed at the corporate level. Thus, by operating as a pseudo-corporation, you would enjoy the multiple advantages of the corporation without the unlimited liability of a proprietorship or partnership. Detailed advantages for handling income of the pseudo-corporation are too numerous to note here, but they make this form of organization highly desirable for corporations with ten or fewer shareholders. A lawyer wise to the formalities and requirements of the IRS code should help you set up a subchapter-S corporation.

Steps to Follow in Incorporating Your Business

Corporations are legal "persons" created under state laws. Since the laws of each state vary, you will find minor variations from these general steps according to the state in which you are incorporating. Note that you need not incorporate your business in the state in which you live or intend to operate.

The Certificate of Incorporation is granted by the Department of State or other state official charged with granting corporate charters. You can obtain a copy of your state's certificate from local stationery stores or from the state official. Information required for the Certificate of Incorporation includes—

● Corporate name. It should not be similar to a name already chartered in the state. Your best bet is to check the list of existing names chartered before selecting one of your own. Further, the name must not be deceptive so as to mislead the public. If in doubt, ask for a preliminary ruling on the suitability of a name by checking with the state official responsible for issuing charters.

● Purposes for which a corporation is formed. Ask your lawyer to help you word this section because some states limit your company's activities strictly to those granted in the certificate. Specific adherence to stated objectives and activities may limit your expansion plans later. In other states, you may describe your planned activities in broad terms which will permit later expansion without modifying the charter.

● Time limit for the corporation. Unless a specific number of years is specified, the corporation is assumed to be formed in perpetuity.

● Names and addresses of at least three of the incorporators. In some states, one of the incorporators must live in the state. In other states, appointment of an in-state agent satisfies this requirement.

● Location of principal office of the corporation within the state. If you choose to incorporate in a state other than the one where your office will be located, you must designate an agent and cite the agent's address. Normally, unless the corporation has specific reasons for doing otherwise, you will probably find it most convenient to incorporate within your own state and cite your home or business location as the principal office in the certificate.

● Maximum amount and type of capital stock which the corporation wishes to issue. Ordinarily, you will provide for more stock than you plan to issue at incorporation. This authorized but unissued stock can be sold later when additional funds are needed. Unless you make provisions for large amounts of stock at the time of incorporation, you must revise the charter later—at additional expense.

● Capital required at incorporation. Your state may require a minimum subscription of cash banked or paid in before a certificate of incorporation is issued. One state requires as little as $500 on deposit, but regulations vary according to state.

● Names of stockholders, the number of shares subscribed to each stockholder, and their addresses must be listed. Interim directors who will serve until the first formal meeting of stockholders must be listed.

● Fees levied by the state vary widely. Fees divide broadly into two categories—fixed minimum fees for filing, recording, etc., and variable fees levied as a percentage of the valuation of shares issued and authorized. The variable fee schedule sometimes leads corporations to seek incorporation in a state other than their principal location.

Bylaws for Operation

Following the award of a Certificate of Incorporation, the stockholders meet to complete the incorporation. The stockholders first elect a Board of Directors to replace interim directors. The Board then appoints officers, (president, vice-president, etc.) to actually run the corporation. In most small corporations, the Board of Directors and the officers comprise the same people. The Board adopts bylaws for guiding the corporation, again in response to state regulations. Bylaws typically cover such items as—

- Location of the principal office and other offices of the corporation.
- Date and location of stockholders' meetings and provisions for calling and holding such meetings.
- Necessary quorum for stockholders' meetings.
- Voting privileges of stockholders.
- Number and method of electing directors and of creating or filling vacancies on the Board of Directors.
- Time and place of directors' meetings and requirements for a quorum.
- Method of selecting officers, their duties, terms of office, and salaries.
- Regulations on stock certificates, their transfer, their control in the company books, and the right to declare dividends.
- Methods for and power to amend the bylaws.

Further Information

These brief directions on choosing a form of business organization and how to incorporate your business may not answer all of your questions. They are intended mainly to advise you of certain problems affecting all businesses. For more information, consult your own lawyer or one of the listed sources. In fact, the technicalities involved with filing for a

Certificate of Incorporation and complying with state regulations on bylaws usually require professional legal assistance. If you do not regularly consult a lawyer, ask your friendly banker for a reference to a lawyer familiar with new business incorporations or call your local bar association for help in locating a lawyer.

The following sources provide further information on business organization and the tax implications of different organizational forms—

● *Managing the Independent Business,* L. Preston, Prentice-Hall, Inc., Englewood Cliffs, New Jersey.

● *Corporations in the Farm Business,* N. G. P. Krausz and Fred L. Mann, College of Agriculture, University of Illinois, Urbana, Ill. Don't let the farm slant throw you off, as most of the contents apply equally to all forms of business.

● "Incorporate and Elect Subchapter-S Pros and Cons for Proprietors, Partners," Arthur B. Willis, *Journal of Taxation,* August, 1959.

● *Organizational Problems of Small Businesses,* Leonard Sarner, revised by Howell C. Mette, Committee on Continuing Legal Education of the American Law Institute, 133 South Street, Philadelphia, Pa., 19104.

WHERE TO GET HELP TO SET UP YOUR OWN BUSINESS

Getting your new business started requires much planning. You need advice on every aspect of your business organization, market research, accounting, facilities planning, and, seemingly, endless others. Sometimes you pay for advice—either through costly experience or from a lawyer or other specialist. But, many sources of eye-popping information are as close as your library or by mail from numerous other sources. This section tells you where to get further information on many of the functions and activities of your new business.

Small Business Administration

Personal counseling on many business problems is available

at the 78 field offices of the Small Business Administration (SBA) located in principal cities in the U.S. You may also apply for financial assistance from the SBA (see Chapter 10). But, probably the most valuable assistance for you is the SBA's publications program. You can acquire a booklet on just about every subject relative to small business enterprise. The SBA's publications program breaks down into two categories—free folders and "for-sale" booklets. The "for-sale" list includes a wealth of information generally broken down into these categories—

● Small business management series—Aimed at improving managerial capabilities with such titles as *Sales Training for the Smaller Manufacturer, The Foreman in Small Industry, A Handbook of Small Business Finance, Insurance and Risk Management for Small Businesses,* plus many more.

● Starting and managing series—These booklets integrate vertically the information needed by someone about to start a specific business. Typical titles include *Starting and Managing a Service Station, Starting and Managing a Swap Shop or Consignment Sale Shop,* and many others.

● Business research series—These in-depth publications include widely varying titles, but the one you should study is *The First Two Years: Problems of Small Firm Growth and Survival.*

● Nonseries publications—These booklets provide specialized information on broad subjects, and include such typical titles as *Export Marketing for Smaller Firms, Managing for Profits,* and others.

● Aids annuals—These compilations of small, individual papers are sold as annuals, hence the name. The aids fall into three categories—management, technical, and marketing. Although the compilations are priced as low as 30 cents, with one costing $1, individual aids can usually be obtained free from one of the field offices of the SBA.

"For-sale" publications offered by the Small Business Administration may be ordered from the Superintendent of Documents, U.S. Government Printing Office, Washington, D.C. 20402.

SCORE Counselors

Service Corps of Retired Executives (SCORE) includes men and women who have successfully completed their own active business careers and volunteered their services to help small businessmen with operating problems. SCORE counselors serve without pay because they appreciate what small business means and has always meant to American free enterprise. SCORE counselors offer their talents, their wisdom, and their experience to any small businessman who needs help.

What kind of help can you get from SCORE? You can ask specific questions, such as "How can I improve my record-keeping system?," call for general advice on how to improve your advertising, marketing, or personnel policies, or consult on specific selling techniques. And the price is right—SCORE counselors work free, although you may be asked to reimburse counselors for their out-of-pocket travel expenses.

How do you get help from SCORE? Your first contact is with a local Small Business Administration field office. The SBA plays only a contact role. The SBA will tell you how to contact a local SCORE chapter or how to reach a counselor with specific talents. You handle the contacts from that point on.

State Aids

Most states offer some form of financial assistance or advice to small businesses, from tax relief for a new business to active help in studying a plant location. States are taking an increasingly active role in sponsoring new business generation activities. One outstanding example is the Regional Development Laboratory sponsored originally by two Philadelphia nonprofit corporations and the Area Redevelopment Administration (now the Economic Development Administration) of the U.S. Dept of Commerce. The nonprofit corporations are the Southeastern Pennsylvania Economic Development Corp. and the West Philadelphia Corp. The aim of the Regional Development Laboratory (RDL) is "...to incubate new ideas for products and services which would create new jobs in southeastern Pennsylvania."

At the time of the report, the RDL had spawned businesses that employed 150 persons with an annual payroll of $1,275,000—almost four times the cost of operating the laboratory. To achieve these objectives the RDL offers—

● A work place away from home—quiet, adequate in size, accessible only to the developer 24 hours a day.

● Access to machine tools and other pieces of laboratory and test equipment.

● Mechanic technician assistance.

● Access to and all privileges of university libraries.

● Secretarial services to write letters, type papers and reports, and take telephone messages.

● Consultation by experts in areas of interest unfamiliar to the developer—not only technical areas, but also in the areas of patents, marketing, finance, and, in fact, in any area which is directly or indirectly related to the development program.

● Contacts for business purposes through all avenues available by virtue of the role played in the southeastern Pennsylvania business community by the two local RDL-sponsoring organizations.

In addition to on-site work space, certain individuals could have access to the RDL through a "commuter research" program. To acquire this kind of help, an inventor or developer first must get his idea approved by a Technical Advisory Board. If his plan is approved, he signs a Service Contract that spells out his obligations and those of the Laboratory. Fees range from less than $10 to about $30 per week, depending on the range of services provided.

Similar not-for-profit aid organizations are being sponsored by universities with financing from some states and various agencies of the Federal Government. Ask your local banker, university public-relations office, state department of business or commerce, or SBA field office for leads to such assistance. This field is growing rapidly, with one major purpose in mind—to develop new industries that will offer jobs within the state or region. For specific information about the Regional

Development Laboratory, address a letter of inquiry to 4040 Locust Street, Philadelphia, Pa. 19104.

Private or Business Sources

A number of business associations, banks, nonprofit organizations, and others offer varied assistance to minority entrepreneurs, small business hopefuls, and individuals. Just a few of these sources of information are noted as follows—

- *Directory of Private Programs for Minority Business Enterprise* is a booklet available free from the Office of Minority Business Enterprise, U.S. Dept. of Commerce, Washington, D.C. The booklet lists city, state, regional, and national organizations offering assistance to minority enterprises and tells briefly what kinds of assistance are available and how you can get it, if you qualify as a minority business enterprise.

- *Small Business Reporter* is a publication issued ten times a year by the Bank of America, San Francisco, California 94120. A year's subscription costs $8.50, but single copies are available free from branch offices of the Bank of America. Single copies of specific reports, such as Apparel Retailing, Auto Parts and Accessory Stores, Coin-Operated Laundries, Recreational Vehicle Parks, and others are also available free from the *Reporter* office. In addition to the business profile series, specific reports on certain functions, such as Advertising, How to Buy or Sell a Business, Financing Small Businesses, Steps in Starting a Business, and others are available—single copies free.

- *Key Business Ratios and Cost of Doing Business* are statistical data sources issued free by Dun & Bradstreet, Inc., 99 Church Street, New York, N.Y. 10007. These statistical compilations offer a wealth of data for ratio analysis for most businesses. From these analyses, you can tell how you are doing and whether your costs are out of line with averages.

- Trade magazines cover practically every business you might consider. Check your library for current and back copies. Trade magazines report on successful operators in your line of activity, cite cost- and labor-saving ideas, keep you posted on legislation pending in Congress, technical developments of interest, new equipment, possible business expansion opportunities, and provide a communication exchange that keeps you current on every facet of development involving your business.

HOW TO SAVE MONEY ON TAXES

Taxes of all kinds, but primarily federal income taxes, affect every business regardless of size. As a small businessman, you should be aware of the continually changing tax regulations and interpretations of the law as they influence your business. Two excellent sources of information are available for modest cost—

 1. *Tax Guide for Small Business,* Internal Revenue Service Publication No. 334 is issued yearly.

 2. *Executive's Tax Report* is published weekly by Prentice-Hall, Inc., Englewood Cliffs, New Jersey, 07632. It includes data and reports on the continuing changes in procedures issued by the Internal Revenue Service and from court decisions.

Rather than spend critical time studying the tax code to become your own tax expert, consider bartering your services for counsel and advice from a specialist. Tax consultants offer individual counsel and service, much like lawyers. Many times tax savings more than pay for the cost of these services.

HOW TO BUILD YOUR OWN TAX-FREE RETIREMENT FUND

Officers and employees of corporations and government organizations have long enjoyed retirement benefits paid for mainly from before-tax dollars. A federal law, popularly known as the Keough Act, provides similar benefits for the self-employed business or professional person. If you are a doctor, lawyer, or owner or partner in an unincorporated business, you qualify—as long as no employers pay any Social Security Tax for you. Under the Keough Act, you can contribute $2,500 or 10 per cent of your self-employed earned income, whichever is less, into a fund each year. For taxable years beginning January, 1968, such contributions are fully tax-deductible—in other words, you set up your retirement fund with before-tax dollars. If your earned income is $25,000, your tax saving on the $2,500 contribution to your own Keough Plan, could amount to more than $1,000, depending on the number of your dependents.

Interest, dividends, and other increments earned by your retirement fund are permitted to build up tax-free until distributed to you. This compounding of earnings without tax means that your retirement fund builds fast. Note these facts about setting up your tax-free retirement fund —

● If you have no employees, you set up your own individual plan. You must, however, include full-time, nonseasonal employees with at least three years' service in your plan on the same basis as your own. (Full-time employees are defined as those who work more than 20 hours per week and at least five months during the year.) Contributions for employees are fully deductible expenses.

● You or any covered employees may voluntarily contribute more nondeductible funds up to the 10 per cent or $2,500 limit. Once these after-tax dollars are in your retirement fund, they are sheltered and may accrue interest or dividends free of tax.

● You may withdraw funds only upon reaching age 59½ and funds must be withdrawn by age 70½. In case of death or disability, retirement funds can be withdrawn immediately. Funds withdrawn before age 59½ will be taxed.

● Your retirement fund must be established as a trust fund with a bank acting as trustee. However, as trustee, the bank must follow your directions for investing the funds—possibly in stocks, bonds, mutual funds, land, or United States Bonds. You enjoy considerable flexibility in directing the investment policy of the trust fund—but you must do it through the bank as trustee.

● Avoid plans which call for investment of your funds in annuities, mutual funds, land, or other possibilities with minimum freedom of action. Settle only for a plan which allows you full freedom of choice for investing your retirement fund contributions and its earnings.

● Not all banks provide trustee services. However, your banker can steer you to a bank that will set up your trust fund, or you can write to The National Bank of Georgia, 34 Peachtree Street, Atlanta, Georgia. The National Bank of Georgia acts as trustee for accounts from all over the United States and is one of the least expensive of the trustees.

INDEX